Toronto Blue Jays 2019

A Baseball Companion

Edited by Patrick Dubuque, Aaron Gleeman and Bret Sayre

Baseball Prospectus

Craig Brown and Dave Pease, Consultant Editors
Rob McQuown and Harry Pavlidis, Statistics Editors

Copyright © 2019 by DIY Baseball, LLC.
All rights reserved

This book or any part thereof may not be reproduced or transmitted in any form or by any means, electronic or mechanical, including photocopying, recording, or by any information storage and retrieval system, without permission in writing from the publisher.

Limit of Liability/Disclaimer of Warranty: While the publisher and the author have used their best efforts in preparing this book, they make no representations or warranties with respect to the accuracy or completeness of the contents of this book and specifically disclaim any implied warranties of merchantability or fitness for a particular purpose. No warranty may be created or extended by sales representatives or written sales materials. The advice and strategies contained herein may not be suitable for your situation. You should consult with a professional where appropriate. Neither the publisher nor the author shall be liable for any loss of profit or any other commercial damages, including but not limited to special, incidental, consequential, or other damages.

Library of Congress Cataloging-in-Publication Data:
paperback
ISBN-13: 978-1-949332-28-5

Project Credits
Cover Design: Kathleen Dyson
Interior Design and Production: Jeff Pease, Dave Pease
Layout: Jeff Pease, Dave Pease

Baseball icon courtesy of Uberux, from https://www.shareicon.net/author/uberux

Ballpark diagram courtesy of Lou Spirito/THIRTY81 Project, https://thirty81project.com/

Manufactured in the United States of America
10 9 8 7 6 5 4 3 2 1

Table of Contents

Foreword v
    Rob Mains

Statistical Introduction vii

Part 1: Team Analysis

Table for Two: Previewing the 2019 Toronto Blue Jays 3
    Nick Dika and Joshua Howsam

Performance Graphs 7

2018 Team Performance 8

2019 Team Projections 9

Team Personnel 10

Rogers Centre Stats 11

Blue Jays Team Analysis 13

Part 2: Player Analysis

Blue Jays Player Analysis 18

Blue Jays Prospects 97

Part 3: Featured Articles

The Hole in The Shift is Fixing Itself 111
    Russell Carleton

The State of the Quality Start 115
    Rob Mains

Heads-Up Hacking—The First Pitch 121
    Matthew Trueblood

A Hymn for the Index Stat 127
    Patrick Dubuque

Index of Names 131

Foreword

Rob Mains

Welcome to this companion of the 2019 Toronto Blue Jays. We at Baseball Prospectus are excited to provide this analysis of the Blue Jays.

Our website, Baseball Prospectus, is a leader in delivering high-quality commentary and data to baseball fans everywhere. To some, those words—commentary and data—appear mutually exclusive. There are people out there who believe that traditional analysis and advanced analytics must run on different paths. But the simplistic narrative of stats vs. traditionalists just isn't true. Every team's analytics department interacts with scouting, development, and major league operations with a common goal: Delivering a championship. New technologies, like radar tracking of pitch speeds and movement, enable talent evaluators to focus on qualitative aspects of pitching like mechanics and pitch sequencing. In-game strategies like infield shifts, based on batters' hit tendencies, help turn balls in play into outs. Hitters use information to adjust their swings to maximize run production.

All these numbers can seem, at best, intimidating, and at worst, counterproductive to the casual fan. Even as technology and analysis have embedded themselves deeply into the way teams run, it can often feel like statistics create a displacement between the viewer and the sport, breaking them out of the action. And yet every fan incorporates the numbers to some degree; stats like batting average and earned run average, so fundamental to how we talk about performance, are actually complicated formulas. They don't bother people because those formulas have become second nature, as easy to translate as the action on the field.

Along the way, new statistics have entered baseball's lexicon. You'll see some of them, like on-base percentage (which measures a batter's ability to get on base via walk, hit batter, or hit), OPS (on-base plus slugging), and average exit velocity (the speed of balls off a hitter's bat) on broadcasts. Others, like DRC+, might well be new to you. Some of them have been well-defined to the public, others haven't. That lack of context has created ambiguity. Fans know that a ball hit 100 mph is scorched, but does that mean extra bases? (Not if it's hit on the ground or high in the air it doesn't.)

For those who are amenable to them, the new statistics can increase the enjoyment and understanding of the game. They can help fans identify when a pitcher is tiring, when a stolen base or a bunt attempt makes sense (and, more often, when it doesn't), or how a team's lineup might be constructed. Websites like Baseball Prospectus add to that understanding by weaving metrics into the narrative of the game. That's the goal of this publication: to take some of the newer, more complicated statistics and make them as intuitive as the ones on the back of old baseball cards.

But you don't need to love analytics to love baseball. The fans at BP who worked together to write this guide are captivated first and foremost by the game itself. We're drawn to Aaron Judge's power, Francisco Lindor's glove, Billy Hamilton's speed and Patrick Corbin's slider and don't need numbers to tell us why they're so mesmerizing. The underlying statistics provide depth to the game that we all love.

We hope you'll find that this guide helps you better understand the Blue Jays. Our analysts have studied the team's major league personnel and its minor league affiliates to identify their strengths and weaknesses, both the obvious ones and those that only a careful dissection of players' performances—yes, including the data—can reveal. You don't need us to tell you who was good and who wasn't in 2018, but our models and writers can help you project how each player is going to perform this year and beyond, and appreciate the greatness of each new game as it unfolds. As in the sport itself, the human and analytic components combine to generate a deeper overall understanding.

Think back to the first time you saw a baseball game on a high-definition TV. You'd grown familiar with how the game looked and felt on a picture tube. But new TV allowed you to see details that you'd never seen before. That's how advanced statistics work. The game itself is why you're here and why you're buying this. (And, for that matter, why we wrote it.) The statistical measures provide the sharper focus, the detail, the depth of knowledge that you didn't have before, generating an overall superior picture. Enjoy the view.

—*Rob Mains is an author of Baseball Prospectus.*

Statistical Introduction

Sports are, fundamentally, a blend of athletic endeavor and storytelling. Baseball, like any other sport, tells its stories in so many ways: in the arc of a game from the stands or a season from the box scores, in photos, or even in numbers. At Baseball Prospectus, we understand that statistics don't replace observation or any of baseball's stories, but complement everything else that makes the game so much fun.

What stats help us with is with patterns and precision, variance and value. This book can help you learn things you may not see from watching a game or hundred, whether it's the path of a career over time or the breadth of the entire MLB. We'd also never ask you to choose between our numbers and the experience of viewing a game from the cheap seats or the comfort of your home; our publication combines running the numbers with observations and wisdom from some of the brightest minds we can find. But if you *do* want to learn more about the numbers beyond what's on the backs of player jerseys, let us help explain.

Offense

At the end of this past year, we've revised our methodology for determining batting value. Long-time readers of Baseball Prospectus will notice that we've retired True Average in favor of a new metric: Deserved Runs Created Plus (DRC+). Developed by Jonathan Judge and our stats team, this statistic measures everything a player does at the plate–reaching base, hitting for power, making outs, and moving runners over–and puts it on a scale where 100 equals league-average performance. A DRC+ of 150 is terrific, a DRC+ of 100 is average, and a DRC+ of 75 means you better be an excellent defender.

DRC+ also does a better job than any of our previous metrics in taking contextual factors into account. The model adjusts for how the park affects performance, but also for things like the talent of the opposing pitcher, value of different types of batted-ball events, league, temperature, and other factors. It's able to describe a player's expected offensive contribution than any other statistic we've found over the years, and also does a better job of predicting future performance as well.

The other aspect of run-scoring is baserunning, which we quantify using Baserunning Runs. BRR not only records the value of stolen bases (or getting caught in the act), but also accounts for a runner's ability to go first to third on a single or advance on a fly ball.

Defense

Where offensive value is *relatively* easy to identify and understand, defensive value is ... not. Over the past dozen years, the sabermetric community has focused mostly on stats based on zone data: a real-live human person records the type of batted ball and estimated landing location, and models are created that give expected outs. From there, you can compare fielders' actual outs to those expected ones. Simple, right?

Unfortunately, zone data has two major issues. First, zone data is recorded by commercial data providers who keep the raw data private unless you pay for it. (All the statistics we build in this book and on our website use public data as inputs.) That hurts our ability to test assumptions or duplicate results. Second, over the years it has become apparent that there's quite a bit of "noise" in zone-based fielding analysis. Sometimes the conclusions drawn from zone data don't hold up to scrutiny, and sometimes the different data provided by different providers don't look anything alike, giving wildly different results. Sometimes the hard-working professional stringers or scorers might unknowingly inflict unconscious bias into the mix: for example good fielders will often be credited with more expected outs despite the data, and ballparks with high press boxes tend to score more line drives than ones with a lower press box.

Enter our Fielding Runs Above Average (FRAA). For most positions, FRAA is built from play-by-play data, which allows us to avoid the subjectivity found in many other fielding metrics. The idea is this: count how many fielding plays are made by a given player and compare that to expected plays for an average fielder at their position (based on pitcher ground-ball tendencies and batter handedness). Then we adjust for park and base-out situations.

When it comes to catchers, our methodology is a little different thanks to the laundry list of responsibilities they're tasked with beyond just, well, catching and throwing the ball. By now you've probably heard about "framing" or the art of making umpires more likely to call balls outside the strike zone for strikes. To put this into one tidy number, we incorporate pitch tracking data (for the years it exists) and adjust for important factors like pitcher, umpire, batter, and home-field advantage using a mixed-model approach. This grants us a number for how many strikes the catcher is personally adding to (or subtracting from) his pitchers' performance ... which we then convert to runs added or lost using linear weights.

Framing is one of the biggest parts of determining catcher value, but we also take into account blocking balls from going past, whether a scorer deems it a passed ball or a wild pitch. We use a similar approach–one that really benefits from the pitch tracking data that tells us what ends up in the dirt and what doesn't. We also include a catcher's ability to prevent stolen bases and how well they field balls in play, and *finally* we come up with our FRAA for catchers.

Pitching

Both pitching and fielding make up the half of baseball that isn't run scoring: run prevention. Separating pitching from fielding is a tough task, and most recent pitching analysis has branched off from Voros McCracken's famous (and controversial) statement, "There is little if any difference among major-league pitchers in their ability to prevent hits on balls hit in the field of play." The research of the analytic community has validated this to some extent, and there are a host of "defense-independent" pitching measures that have been developed to try and extricate the effect of the defense behind a hurler from the pitcher's work.

Our solution to this quandry is Deserved Run Average (DRA), our core pitching metric. DRA looks like earned run average (ERA), the tried-and-true pitching stat you've seen on every baseball broadcast or box score from the past century, but it's very different. To start, DRA takes an event-by-event look at what the pitchers does, and adjusts the value of that event based on different environmental factors like park, batter, catcher, umpire, base-out situation, run differential, inning, defense, home field advantage, pitcher role, and temperature. That mixed model gives us a pitcher's expected contribution, similar to what we do for our DRC+ model for hitters and FRAA model for catchers. (Oh, and we also consider the pitcher's effect on basestealing and on balls getting past the catcher.)

It's important to note that DRA is set to the scale of runs allowed per nine innings (RA9) instead of ERA, which makes DRA's scale slightly higher than ERA's. The reason for this is because ERA tends to overrate three types of pitchers:

1. Pitchers who play in parks where scorers hand out more errors. Official scorers differ significantly in the frequency at which they assign errors to fielders.
2. Ground-ball pitchers, because a substantial proportion of errors occur on grounders.
3. Pitchers who aren't very good. Better pitchers often allow fewer unearned runs than bad pitchers, because good pitchers tend to find ways to get out of jams.

Since the last time you picked up an edition of this book, we've also made a few minor changes to DRA to make it better. Recent research into "tunneling"–the act of throwing consecutive pitches that appear similar from a batter's point of view until after the swing decision point–data has given us a new contextual factor to account for in DRA: plate distance. This refers to the distance between successive pitches as they approach the plate, and while it has a smaller effect than factors like velocity or whiff rate, it still can help explain pitcher strikeout rate in our model.

New Pitching Metrics for 2019

We're including a few "new" pitching metrics for 2019's suite of Baseball Prospectus publications, but you may be familiar with them if you've spent time scouring the internet for stats.

Fastball Percentage

Our fastball percentage (FB%) statistic measures how frequently a pitcher throws a pitch classified as a "fastball," measured as a percentage of overall pitches thrown. We qualify three types of fastballs:

1. The traditional four-seam fastball;
2. The two-seam fastball or sinker;
3. "Hard cutters," which are pitches that have the movement profile of a cut fastball and are used as the pitcher's primary offering or in place of a more traditional fastball.

For example, a pitcher with a FB% of 67 throws any combination of these three pitches about two-thirds of the time.

Whiff Rate

Everybody loves a swing and a miss, and whiff rate (WHF) measures how frequently pitchers induce a swinging strike. To calculate WHF, we add up all the pitches thrown that ended with a swinging strike, then divide that number by a pitcher's total pitches thrown. Most often, high whiff rates correlate with high strikeout rates (and overall effective pitcher performance).

Called Strike Probability

Called Strike Probability (CSP) is a number that represents the likelihood that all of a pitcher's pitches will be called a strike while controlling for location, pitcher and batter handedness, umpire and count. Here's how it works: on each pitch, our model determines how many times (out of 100) that a similar pitch was called for a strike given those factors mentioned above, and when normalized for each batter's strike zone. Then we average the CSP for all pitches thrown by a pitcher in a season, and that gives us the yearly CSP percentage you see in the stats boxes.

As you might imagine, pitchers with a higher CSP are more likely to work in the zone, where pitchers with a lower CSP are likely locating their pitches outside the normal strike zone, for better or for worse.

Projections

Many of you aren't turning to this book just for a look at what a player has done, but for a look at what a player is going to do: the PECOTA projections. PECOTA, initially developed by Nate Silver (who has moved on to greater fame as a political analyst), consists of three parts:

1. Major-league equivalencies, which use minor-league statistics to project how a player will perform in the major leagues;
2. Baseline forecasts, which use weighted averages and regression to the mean to estimate a player's current true talent level; and
3. Aging curves, which uses the career paths of comparable players to estimate how a player's statistics are likely to change over time.

With all those important things covered, let's take a look at what's in the book this year.

Team Prospectus

You bought this book to learn more about your favorite (or maybe least-favorite, who are we to judge?) team, so let's talk about them. After a thoughtful preview of the 2019 season, you'll be presented with our Team Prospectus. This outlines many of the key statistics for each team's 2018 season, as well as a very inviting stadium diagram.

First you'll find the Performance Graphs page. The first is the 2018 Hit List Ranking. This shows our Hit List Rank for the team on each day of the 2018 season and is intended to give you a picture of the ups and downs of the team's season, including their highest and lowest ranks of the year. Hit List Rank measures overall team performance and drives the Hit List Power Rankings at the baseballprospectus.com website.

The second graph is Committed Payroll and helps you see how the team's payroll has compared to the MLB and divisional average payrolls over time. Payroll figures are currents as of January 1, 2019; with so many free agents still unsigned as of this writing, the final 2018 figure will likely be significantly different for many teams. (In the meantime, you can always find the most current data at Baseball Prospectus' Cot's Baseball Contracts page.)

Toronto Blue Jays 2019

The third graph is Farm System Ranking and displays how the Baseball Prospectus prospect team has ranked the organization's farm system since 2007. It also indicates the highest and lowest ranks that the farm system achieved over that time.

We start the Team Performance page with the squad's unadjusted and third-order 2018 win-loss records, presented in divisional context. We then list the three highest performing hitters and pitchers by WARP for 2018. Beneath that are a host of other team statistics. **Pythag** presents an adjusted 2018 winning percentage, calculated by taking runs scored per game (**RS/G**) and runs allowed per game (**RA/G**) for the team, and running them through a version of Bill James' Pythagorean formula that was refined and improved by David Smyth and Brandon Heipp. (The formula is called "Pythagenpat," which is equally fun to type and to say.)

Next up is **DRC+**, described earlier, to indicate the overall hitting ability of the team either above or below league-average. Run prevention on the pitching side is covered by **DRA** (also mentioned earlier) and another metric: Fielding Independent Pitching (**FIP**), which calculates another ERA-like statistic based on strikeouts, walks, and home runs recorded. Defensive Efficiency Rating (**DER**) tells us the percentage of balls in play turned into outs for the team, and is a quick fielding shorthand that rounds out run prevention.

After that, we have several measures related to roster composition, as opposed to on-field performance. **B-Age** and **P-Age** tell us the average age of a team's batters and pitchers, respectively. **Salary** is the combined team payroll for all on-field players, and Doug Pappas' Marginal Dollars per Marginal Win (**M$/MW**) tells us how much money a team spent to earn production above replacement level.

Ending this batch of statistics is the number of disabled list days a team had over the season (**DL Days**) and the amount of salary paid to players on the disabled list (**$ on DL**); this final number is expressed as a percentage of total payroll.

Next to each of these stats, we've listed each team's MLB rank in that category from 1st to 30th. In this, 1st always indicates a positive outcome and 30th a negative outcome, except in the case of salary–1st is highest.

The Team Projections page is intended to convey the team's operational capacity entering the 2019 season. We start with the team's PECOTA projected record for 2019, again in divisional context. The **+/-** column indicates how many more or less wins the team is projected to get than they got in 2018. We then list the three highest projected hitters and pitchers by WARP for 2018. A brief farm system summary follows, with the team's top prospect and number of BP Top 101 Prospects. Finally, we list the key new players and departed players, along with their 2019 projected WARP.

Alex Bregman 3B

Born: 03/30/94   Age: 25   Bats: R   Throws: R
Height: 6'0"   Weight: 180   Origin: Round 1, 2015 Draft (#2 overall)

YEAR	TEAM	LVL	AGE	PA	R	2B	3B	HR	RBI	BB	K	SB	CS	AVG/OBP/SLG
2016	CCH	AA	22	285	54	16	2	14	46	42	26	5	3	.297/.415/.559
2016	FRE	AAA	22	83	17	6	0	6	15	5	12	2	1	.333/.373/.641
2016	HOU	MLB	22	217	31	13	3	8	34	15	52	2	0	.264/.313/.478
2017	HOU	MLB	23	626	88	39	5	19	71	55	97	17	5	.284/.352/.475
2018	HOU	MLB	24	705	105	51	1	31	103	96	85	10	4	.286/.394/.532
2019	HOU	MLB	25	675	96	38	3	23	78	73	107	12	4	.272/.359/.463

Breakout: 6%   Improve: 52%   Collapse: 5%   Attrition: 2%   MLB: 100%
Comparables: Anthony Rendon, David Wright, Pablo Sandoval

YEAR	TEAM	LVL	AGE	PA	DRC+	VORP	BABIP	BRR	FRAA	WARP
2016	CCH	AA	22	285	172	38.9	.286	1.6	SS(51): -3.4, 3B(11): 1.4	2.7
2016	FRE	AAA	22	83	161	10.0	.333	-1.2	SS(14): 2.1, LF(3): -0.1	0.8
2016	HOU	MLB	22	217	107	9.6	.317	0.5	3B(40): 0.9, SS(6): -0.1	1.1
2017	HOU	MLB	23	626	114	34.7	.311	-1.5	3B(132): 8.7, SS(30): -2.9	3.9
2018	HOU	MLB	24	705	150	72.6	.289	-1.6	3B(136): 5.4, SS(28): -0.4	7.4
2019	HOU	MLB	25	675	125	37.3	.295	0.0	3B 7, SS 0	4.6

After the projections page, we share a few items about the team's home ballpark. There's the aforementioned diagram of the park's dimensions (including distances to the outfield wall), a few important biographical facts about the stadium, a graphic showing the height of the wall from the left-field pole to the right-field pole, and a table showing three-year park factors for the stadium. The park factors are displayed as indexes where 100 is average, 110 means that the park inflates the statistic in question by 10 percent, and 90 means that the park deflates the statistic in question by 10 percent.

Following the ballpark page, we have a **Personnel** section that lists many of the important decision-makers and upper-level field and operations staff members for the franchise, as well as any former Baseball Prospectus staff members who are currently part of the organization.

Position Players

After all that information and a thoughtful bylined essay covering each team, we present our player comments. Each player is listed with the major-league team who employed him as of early January 2019. If a player changed teams after that point via free agency, trade, or any other method, you'll be able to find them in the book for their previous squad.

First, we cover biographical information (age is as of June 30, 2019) before moving onto the stats themselves. Our statistic columns include standard identifying information like **YEAR**, **TEAM**, **LVL** (level of affiliated play) and **AGE** before getting into the numbers. Next, we provide raw, unstranslated numbers like you might find on the back of your dad's baseball cards: **PA** (plate appearances), **R** (runs), **2B** (doubles), **3B** (triples), **HR** (home runs), **RBI** (runs batted in), **BB** (walks), **K** (strikeouts), **SB** (stolen bases) and **CS** (caught stealing). Then we have unadjusted "slash" statistics: **AVG** (batting average), **OBP** (on-base percentage) and **SLG** (slugging percentage).

Just below the stats box is **PECOTA** data, which is discussed further in a following section. After that, it's on to a pithy and always-informative comment written by a member of the Baseball Prospectus staff, before we cover more stats.

The second text box repeats YEAR, TEAM, LVL, AGE, and PA, then moves on to **DRC+** (Deserved Runs Created Plus), which we described earlier as total offensive expected contribution compared to the league average. Next, one of our oldest active metrics, **VORP** (Value Over Replacement Player), considers offensive production, position and plate appearances. In essence, it is the number of runs contributed beyond what a replacement-level player at the same position would contribute if given the same percentage of team plate appearances. VORP does not consider the quality of a player's defense.

BABIP (batting average on balls in play) tells us how often a ball in play fell for a hit, and can help us identify whether a batter may have been lucky or not … but note that high BABIPs also tend to follow the great hitters of our time, as well as speedy singles hitters who put the ball on the ground.

The next item is **BRR** (Baserunning Runs), which covers all of a player's baserunning accomplishments which includes (but isn't limited to) swiped bags and failed attempts. Next is **FRAA** (Fielding Runs Above Average), which also includes the number of games previously played at each position noted in parentheses. Multi-position players have only their two most frequent positions listed here, but their total FRAA number reflects all positions played.

Our last column here is **WARP** (Wins Above Replacement Player). WARP estimates the total value of a player, which means for hitters it takes into account hitting runs above average (calculated using the DRC+ model), BRR and FRAA. Then, it makes an adjustment for positions played and gives the player a credit for plate appearances based upon the difference between "replacement level"¬–which is derived from the quality of players added to a team's roster after the start of the season¬–and the league average.

Catchers

Catchers are a special breed, and thus they have earned their own separate box which displays some of the defensive metrics that we've built just for them. As an example, let's check out J.T. Realmuto.

YEAR	TEAM	P. COUNT	FRM RUNS	BLK RUNS	THRW RUNS	TOT RUNS
2016	MIA	18935	-8.5	1.8	2.1	-5.6
2017	MIA	18959	5.3	1.7	1.0	9.1
2018	MIA	16399	-0.4	0.9	0.1	0.4
2019	PHI	18448	-1.4	1.5	0.7	0.8

The **YEAR** and **TEAM** columns match what you'd find in the other stat box. **P. COUNT** indicates the number of pitches thrown while the catcher was behind the plate, including swinging strikes, fouls, and balls in play. **FRM RUNS** is the total run value the catcher provided (or cost) his team by influencing the umpire to call strikes where other catchers did not. **BLK RUNS** expresses the total run value above or below average for the catcher's ability to prevent wild pitches and passed balls. **THRW RUNS** is calculated using a similar model as the previous two statistics, and it measures a catcher's ability to throw out basestealers but also to dissuade them from testing his arm in the first place. It takes into account factors like the pitcher (including his delivery and pickoff move) and baserunner (who could be as fast as Billy Hamilton or as slow as Yonder Alonso). **TOT RUNS** is the sum of all of the previous three statistics.

Pitchers

Let's give our pitchers a turn, using 2018 NL Cy Young winner Jacob deGrom as our example. Take a look at his first stat block: the first line and the **YEAR**, **TEAM**, **LVL** and **AGE** columns are the same as in the position player example earlier.

Here too, we have a series of columns that display raw, unadjusted statistics compiled by the pitcher over the course of a season: **W** (wins), **L** (losses), **SV** (saves), **G** (games pitched), **GS** (games started), **IP** (innings pitched), **H** (hits allowed) and **HR** (home runs allowed). Next we have two statistics that are rates: **BB/9** (walks per nine innings) and **K/9** (strikeouts per nine innings), before returning to the unadjusted **K** (strikeouts).

Next up is **GB%** (ground ball percentage), which is the percentage of all batted balls that were hit in the ground, including both outs and hits. Remember, this is based on observational data and subject to human error, so please approach this with a healthy dose of skepticism.

BABIP (batting average on balls in play) is calculated using the same methodology as it is for position players, but it often tells us more about a pitcher than it does a hitter. With pitchers, a high BABIP is often due to poor defense or bad luck, and can often be an indicator of potential rebound, and a low BABIP may be cause to expect performance regression. (A typical league-average BABIP is close to .290-.300.)

After a witty 150ish words on the player like only Baseball Prospectus's staff can provide, it's on to that second stat block, which repeats the YEAR, TEAM, LVL, and AGE columns. The metrics **WHIP** (walks plus hits per inning pitched) and **ERA**

Toronto Blue Jays 2019

(earned run average) are old standbys: WHIP measures walks and hits allowed on a per-inning basis, while ERA measures earned runs on a nine-inning basis. Neither of these stats are translated or adjusted.

DRA (Deserved Run Average) was described at length earlier, and measures how many runs the pitcher "deserved" to allow per nine innings. Please note that since we lack all the data points that would make for a "real" DRA for minor-league events, the DRA displayed for minor league partial-seasons is based off of different data. (That data is a modified version of our cFIP metric, which you can find more information about on our website.)

Jacob deGrom RHP
Born: 06/19/88   Age: 31   Bats: L   Throws: R
Height: 6'4"   Weight: 180   Origin: Round 9, 2010 Draft (#272 overall)

YEAR	TEAM	LVL	AGE	W	L	SV	G	GS	IP	H	HR	BB/9	K/9	K	GB%	BABIP
2016	NYN	MLB	28	7	8	0	24	24	148	142	15	2.2	8.7	143	47%	.312
2017	NYN	MLB	29	15	10	0	31	31	201^1	180	28	2.6	10.7	239	48%	.305
2018	NYN	MLB	30	10	9	0	32	32	217	152	10	1.9	11.2	269	48%	.281
2019	NYN	MLB	31	13	9	0	31	31	186	145	18	2.3	10.7	221	46%	.286

Breakout: 8%   Improve: 29%   Collapse: 28%   Attrition: 6%   MLB: 85%
Comparables: Erik Bedard, A.J. Burnett, CC Sabathia

YEAR	TEAM	LVL	AGE	WHIP	ERA	DRA	WARP	MPH	FB%	WHF	CSP
2016	NYN	MLB	28	1.20	3.04	3.30	3.5	96.3	59.6	12.1	47.2
2017	NYN	MLB	29	1.19	3.53	3.02	5.7	97.2	55.5	14.5	49.5
2018	NYN	MLB	30	0.91	1.70	2.09	8.0	98.2	52.1	16.3	48.4
2019	NYN	MLB	31	1.02	2.91	3.23	3.9	96.6	54.5	14.8	48.2

Just like with hitters, **WARP** (Wins Above Replacement Player) is a total value metric that puts pitchers of all stripes on the same scale as position players. We use DRA as the primary input for our calculation of WARP. You might notice that relief pitchers (due to their limited innings) may have a lower WARP than you were expecting or than you might see in other WARP-like metrics. WARP does not take leverage into account, just the actions a pitcher performs and the expected value of those actions ... which ends up judging high-leverage relief pitchers differently than you might imagine given their prestige and market value.

MPH gives you the pitcher's 95th percentile velocity for the noted season, in order to give you an idea of what the *peak* fastball velocity a pitcher possesses. Since this comes from our pitch tracking data, it is not publicly available for minor-league pitchers.

Finally, we display the three new pitching metrics we described earlier. **FB%** (fastball percentage) gives you the percentage of fastballs thrown out of all pitches. **WhiffRt** (whiff rate) tells you the percentage of swinging strikes induced out of all pitches. **CS Prob** (called strike probability) expresses the likelihood of all pitches thrown to result in a called strike, after controlling for factors like handedness, umpire, pitch type, count, and location.

PECOTA

All players have PECOTA projections for 2019, as well as a set of other numbers that describe the performance of comparable players according to PECOTA. All projections for 2019 are for the player at the date we went to press in early January and are projected into the league and park context as indicated by the team abbreviation. All PECOTA projected statistics represent a player's projected major-league performance.

The numbers beneath the player's stats–Breakout, Improve, Collapse, Attrition–are part and parcel of the PECOTA projections. They estimate the likelihood of changes in performance relative to the player's previously-established level of production, based on the performance of comparable players:

Breakout Rate is the percent change that a player's production will improve by at least 20 percent relative to the weighted average of his performance over his most recent seasons.

Improve Rate is the percent chance that a player's production will improve at all relative to his baseline performance. A player who is expected to perform just the same as he has in the recent past will have an Improve Rate of 50 percent.

Collapse Rate is the percent chance that a position player's production will decline by at least 25 percent relative to his baseline performance.

Attrition Rate operates on playing time rather than performance. Specifically, it measures the likelihood that a player's playing time will decrease by at least 50 percent relative to his established level.

Breakout Rate and Collapse Rate can sometimes be counterintuitive for players who have already experienced a radical change in performance level. It's also worth noting that the projected decline in a player's rate performances might not be indicative of an expected decline in underlying ability or skill, but could just be an anticipated correction following a breakout season.

MLB% is the percentage of similar players who played in the major leagues in their relevant season.

The final pieces of information are the player's three highest-scoring comparable players as determined by PECOTA. All comparables represent a snapshot of how the listed player was performing at the same age as the current player, so if a 23-year-old pitcher is compared to Bartolo Colon, he's actually being compared to a 23-year-old Colon, not the version that pitched for the Rangers in 2018, nor to Colon's career as a whole.

Toronto Blue Jays 2019

A few points about pitcher projections. First, we aren't yet projecting peak velocity, so that column will be blank in the PECOTA lines. Second, projecting DRA is trickier than evaluating past performance, because it is unclear how deserving each pitcher will be of his anticipated outcomes. However, we know that another DRA-related statistic–contextual FIP or cFIP–estimates future run scoring very well. So for PECOTA, the projected DRA figures you see are based on the past cFIPs generated by the pitcher and comparable players over time, along with the other factors described above.

Lineouts

In each chapter's Lineouts section, you'll find abbreviated text comments, as well as most of same information you'd find in our full player comments. We limit the stats boxes in this section to only including the 2018 information for each player.

Exclusive Player Visualizations

In our constant battle to provide you with new and interesting baseball content you can't find anywhere else, we've added a trio of data visualizations to each hitter's entry in these books and a pair of visualizations for each pitcher.

For hitters, you'll find three new infographics. The first is each player's **Batted Ball Distribution**, which displays the five major sections of the field: LF (left), LCF (left center), CF (center), RCF (right center), and RF (right). The percentage indicated tells us what percentage of batted balls from that hitter fell within that part of the field during the 2018 season. We've also included the hitter's slugging percentage on balls in play (also called **SLGCON**) for that part of the field.

You'll also see two heatmaps: **Strike Zone vs LHP** and **Strike Zone vs RHP**. These heat maps represent a view of the strike zone from behind the catcher. Areas where there is a darker coloration represent the places where a higher percentage of pitches resulted in hits. In other words, the heatmap represents a hitter's "sweet spots" for getting hits against either left-handed or right-handed pitchers, depending on the image.

Pitchers get two images that help explain what their pitches look like from a hitter's perspective: **Pitch Shape vs LHH** and **Pitch Shape vs RHH**. These images show you the shape and the "tunneling" effect of each pitcher's offerings from the batter's perspective. For each type of pitch that a pitcher throws (represented by an indicator shape), there's a set of dots indicating the flight path, where each dot represents a 0.01-second interval. This maps the average trajectory and speed of an offering, ending where the ball crosses the plate. The solid black box represents the regular strike zone, while the gray contour lines indicate the range of locations that a pitcher typically works in.

Below the image, we provide a bit more detailed information about each pitcher's average offering in the **Pitch Types** box. Here, we also list each of the pitcher's major offerings under the **Type** column.

- **Fastballs** (which usually refers to the four-seam variation)
- **Sinkers** and/or two-seam fastballs
- **Cutters** (which could include "hard" cutters like cut fastballs and "soft" cutters that resemble hard sliders)
- **Changeups** (not including most splitters)
- **Splitters** (split-fingered pitches, forkballs, and some split-changes)
- **Sliders** and/or slurves
- **Curveballs** (including spike-curveballs and knuckle-curveballs, as well as some slurvy curves)
- **Slow curveballs** and/or eephus pitches
- **Knuckleballs**
- **Screwballs**

The **Freq** column indicates the percentage of overall pitches that fall into each of those type categories; if a pitcher has a 16.55% score for changeups, then that's the percent of all pitches that he throws as changeups. **Velo** is exactly what you think it is: the average miles per hour for each pitch type. **H Mov** is the number of inches of horizontal movement on the average pitch of that type, while **V Mov** is the number of inches of vertical movement on the average pitch of that type. (At Baseball Prospectus, we measure this over the long flight of the ball and include gravity into the V Mov number in order to give you the most realistic representation of what the pitch *actually* does.)

If you're wondering about the second number in brackets, that's the index for that velocity or movement compared to the league average. Like DRC+, a score of 100 means that the speed or movement is about the same as league average, while a higher score means that there's higher velocity or movement than the league average. Numbers below 100 indicate less velocity or movement than the league average.

Part 1: Team Analysis

Table for Two: Previewing the 2019 Toronto Blue Jays

Nick Dika and Joshua Howsam

Who is Toronto's breakout player for 2019?

NICK DIKA: In the last six months the Jays have traded Josh Donaldson and Russell Martin, along with releasing Troy Tulowitzki. The rebuild is officially on in Toronto. Josh, are you excited to see the kids play in 2019 and who do you see as a potential candidate to break out?

JOSH HOWSAM: It certainly is the end of an era. And an unpleasantly short one at that. I'm not really overly excited to see any of the kids that will actually be on the opening day roster, though (stupid service time manipulation). Well, at least not in 2019 so much. PECOTA doesn't exactly paint a rosy picture of the young talent, with Lourdes Gurriel projected for the best season at a lowly 1.5 WARP. And while most people would pick him in this category, it's hard to argue that he'll do better than last year's 156 PA sample.

Brandon Drury is someone I'm optimistic about, however. His minor league numbers still show a lot of talent and he should get significant playing time. However, I still think the "future" that we're all excited about is still another year away. There will be some ugly growing pains.

NICK: I'm not willing to completely give up on Aaron Sanchez yet. The blister injuries are troubling but with his arsenal, he has the potential to be a high-number two starting pitcher. If he can get his walk/blister issues under control, the fastball/curve/change combo should help him keep his ERA under 4.00.

JOSH: Sanchez is so puzzling. His stuff is incredible, but he's so reliant on ground ball contact—like Marcus Stroman—that I think the Blue Jays infield defence lowers his performance ceiling even after adding Freddy Galvis. And I guess it wouldn't exactly be a breakout, but with his problems of late it would feel like one for sure.

I think there is one player that we can agree is most likely to breakout but won't even be around on Opening Day. I'm surprised it even took four paragraphs to talk about him, but the answer has to be Vladimir Guerrero Jr, right?

NICK: He's the best prospect in Blue Jays' history. PECOTA and scouts alike are projecting him to be an impact bat immediately.

JOSH: That's the craziest part. PECOTA is projecting him to be the 10th best hitter in baseball by DRC+ and it seems absolutely plausible. If he comes close to that it probably won't *feel* like a breakout because of his hype, but it will certainly be one heck of a coming-out party. It's crazy that we're this excited about a guy who won't even be on the roster because he "needs to work on his defense."

NICK: On his defense, I'm not convinced we need to write him off as a DH just yet. He's only 20, hasn't been playing the infield that long, and has apparently made strides defensively. Remember people thought Nolan Arenado couldn't stick at third base. I'm not saying he's going to be an elite defender, but I'm still cautiously optimistic that he can be a corner infielder for the bulk of his major league career.

How will this team end up, and what kind of path will they take to get there?

NICK: The odds of this team contending are long. The offence was solid last season and should remain at least average with the addition of Guerrero Jr. and some of the potential improvements (Danny Jansen, Billy McKinney, Brandon Drury) but the real area of concern is pitching.

JOSH: It makes the addition of Clayton Richard to the rotation that much more puzzling (yet another of their outlier fastball projects). A high contact rate in the AL East with this defensive group isn't exactly a recipe for success. Matt Shoemaker is actually the one who interests me the most. He has never really stayed healthy, but he has posted two sub-4.00 DRA seasons (and ERA, though not the same two). If he can actually last for 160 or so innings, he could provide a ton of value to a transitional rotation. If not, at least the pen isn't that bad?

NICK: It shouldn't be. But a solid-but-not-spectacular bullpen is still going to struggle if they are being called into duty in the fourth or fifth inning three times a week.

JOSH: You think the rotation is THAT bad?

NICK: Aside from Sanchez and Stroman (and like you said, both are ground ball-reliant) there's a whole lot of low ceiling starters in both the Blue Jays' major and high minor league rotations. Mix that with the very talented offenses in the AL East....

JOSH: I agree, but at least Ryan Borucki (there's that outlier fastball movement again) and a few of those depth arms should be able to give them five innings most times out. But if not, a relief corps of Ken Giles, David Phelps, Ryan Tepera, John Axford, David Paulino (who has serious upside if healthy) and then some combination of Joe Biagini, Tim Mayza, Julian Merryweather or Trent Thornton should provide enough multi-inning relievers to weather some tough storms. And we haven't even talked about the potential for former Tampa Bay Ray Charlie Montoyo to use openers!

NICK: If the Jays make any noise whatsoever (and I think for this group that means hanging in the second Wild Card race at the very most), it's going to be because their pitching staff seriously over-performed.

How did the team approach the offseason, and did they do well given their aims?

JOSH: Given the state of the roster at the end of the year, are you at all surprised with the way the Jays' offseason has gone thus far: a few relievers, a depth starter or two and a mediocre shortstop?

NICK: I think the acquisitions fit their current MO – which is to provide some cover in case the Jays' young players (Gurriel, Sean Reid-Foley, Ryan Borucki) can't perform well enough to hold major league jobs. Guys like Matt Shoemaker and Freddy Galvis provide depth but I don't think they're going to stop any of the younger players from winning or taking their jobs, either. The Jays have made a point of acquiring a lot of players that project in that 1-2.5 WARP range over the last several seasons: Randal Grichuk, Teoscar Hernandez, Brandon Drury, Billy McKinney—do you see any of them being able to outperform their projections and become a player the club can build around? Because I think that is what they Jays are hoping for....

JOSH: I'm not 100 percent sure that's actually the goal. It almost seems like they want a floor of decent players to surround their stars with. In the past we've seen this team tank because the quality of its backups was especially poor. The Jays tried to rectify that last year with better depth, but their stars were no good. The hope here seems to be that a few solid surrounding pieces are enough when propped up by the star power from Vlad and Bo and... hopefully someone else.

I'd say they accomplished that with so many players for so many positions. As to your question, I think that Grichuk has the best chance to become someone that transitions from complementary piece to core asset if the Blue Jays eventually move on from Kevin Pillar. Grichuk has been shown capable of handling CF and his usual offense in the middle of the diamond would be pretty valuable. With even a little bit more of post-April 2018 Grichuk and less of his 2017 production, he could be quite useful.

NICK: I'm a little more convinced Grichuk is what he is. He's been remarkably consistent over the past three seasons and unfortunately, that means someone who rarely walks and frequently strikes out. I can't see him tapping into his hard hit rates unless he changes his plate approach. In terms of star power and core pieces, you forgot to mention Danny Jansen—the Jays traded Russell Martin to the Dodgers this offseason so they could clear a path to playing time for the young catcher. With the state of catching, I think he could be a star too: Vlad Jr. wasn't the only Jays' prospect who walked as much as he struck out in the high minors the past two seasons.

JOSH: This is one of the more interesting cases. I happen to think that Jansen is the most likely Blue Jays prospect to outperform his PECOTA projections... on the offensive side. In addition to what you highlighted, we're talking about a guy that put up a 137 DRC+ in Buffalo last year and approximately 150 across three levels of the minors in 2017. But the reason I didn't list him above is because of that defensive projection (-11.3 FRAA. YIKES!). Catchers stink, but with Jansen's poor arm, he'll have to either absolutely mash or vastly improve on what the stats think of his framing last year to become a star. If that happens, the Jays might have enough top-level talent for their depth to make them competitive in the future.

How does this team approach winning differently from other teams, and how does it shape its identity?

NICK: Speaking of Jansen's potential development, the Jays' front office has publicly made a point of focusing on player development, and we have seen improvements from guys in the system over the last two seasons (Jansen, Sean Reid-Foley), is the Atkins/Shapiro front office shaping it's identity as a cutting edge player development organization?

JOSH: I think that would be hard to claim, as we've seen some other clubs absolutely flourish in this area, but there's no doubt that this is a huge focus of the front office. If they're going to win, it's going to be because of their farm system. From focusing on analytics with the hiring a couple of former Driveline Baseball employees to trying to improve culture by taking prospects and putting them through Army Ranger training, they're clearly doing everything they can to make sure the pipeline keeps producing.

I think it says a lot that we're talking about development down the road while attempting to discuss this upcoming season, because this really does seem to be a transition year. The approach to contending this year definitely seems to be hoping and praying for health and improvement. In other words, trying to be the 2018 Rays.

NICK: Even with Vlad, I still see the Jays as a 75-80 win team this season, even if some things do break right. We've seen Mike Trout play on enough mediocre teams to know that even Vlad Jr. on his own can't save a team. I predict a 77-85 season for the Jays in 2019.

JOSH: Yeah, it's going to be rough. I think this year will tell us a lot about the next three of four. If Vlad, Bo, Gurriel, Jansen and a couple of young arms take steps forward, the team could really go for it in 2020 and beyond. If even a few of those guys stagnate, it could be a long few years in the cold. So call up Vlad and let us share in his unbridled joy and watch some missiles hit the Flight Deck.

Performance Graphs

2018 Hit List Ranking

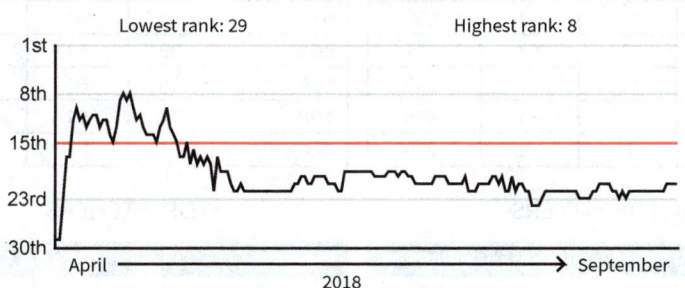

Committed Payroll (in millions)

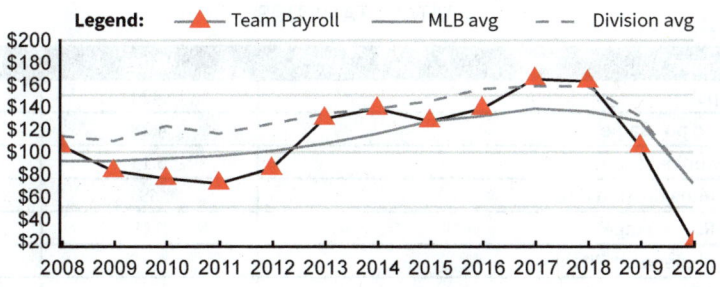

Farm System Ranking

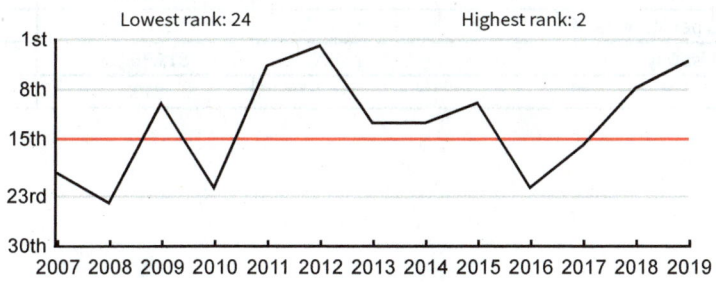

2018 Team Performance

ACTUAL STANDINGS

Team	W	L	Pct
BOS	108	54	.666
NYA	100	62	.617
TBA	90	72	.555
TOR	**73**	**89**	**.450**
BAL	47	115	.290

THIRD-ORDER STANDINGS

Team	W	L	Pct
NYA	99	63	.611
BOS	99	63	.611
TBA	98	64	.604
TOR	**70**	**92**	**.432**
BAL	54	108	.333

TOP HITTERS

Player	WARP
Kevin Pillar	2.8
Randal Grichuk	1.9
Russell Martin	1.7

TOP PITCHERS

Player	WARP
Marcus Stroman	1.3
Tyler Clippard	1.1
J.A. Happ	1

VITAL STATISTICS

Statistic Name	Value	Rank
Pythagenpat	.424	23rd
Runs Scored per Game	4.38	17th
Runs Allowed per Game	5.14	26th
Deserved Runs Created Plus	99	10th
Deserved Run Average	5.18	25th
Fielding Independent Pitching	4.56	24th
Defensive Efficiency Rating	.694	28th
Batter Age	29.0	25th
Pitcher Age	29.2	23rd
Salary	$162.0M	8th
Marginal $ per Marginal Win	$6.1M	6th
Disabled List Days	$1,236.0M	15th
$ on DL	31%	29th

2019 Team Projections

PROJECTED STANDINGS

Team	W	L	Pct	+/-
NYA	96	66	.592	-4
BOS	90	72	.555	-18
TBA	85	77	.524	-5
TOR	**76**	**86**	**.469**	**+3**
BAL	57	105	.351	+10

TOP PROJECTED HITTERS

Player	WARP
Vladimir Guerrero Jr.	3.1
Randal Grichuk	1.8
Justin Smoak	1.6

TOP PROJECTED PITCHERS

Player	WARP
Marcus Stroman	2.5
Aaron Sanchez	1.2
Matt Shoemaker	1.2

FARM SYSTEM REPORT

Top Prospect	Number of Top 101 Prospects
Vladimir Guerrero Jr., #1	4

KEY DEDUCTIONS

Player	WARP
Aledmys Diaz	0.8
Russell Martin	0.6
Taylor Guerrieri	0.4

KEY ADDITIONS

Player	WARP
Matt Shoemaker	1.2
Clayton Richard	0.8
Freddy Galvis	0.5
Clay Buchholz	0.3
Bud Norris	0.3

Team Personnel

President
Mark Shapiro

General Manager
Ross Atkins

VP, Baseball Operations
Ben Cherington

Assistant General Manager
Tony LaCava

Assistant General Manager
Andrew Tinnish

Assistant General Manager
Joe Sheehan

Manager
Charlie Montoyo

BP Alumni
Matt Bishoff

Rogers Centre Stats

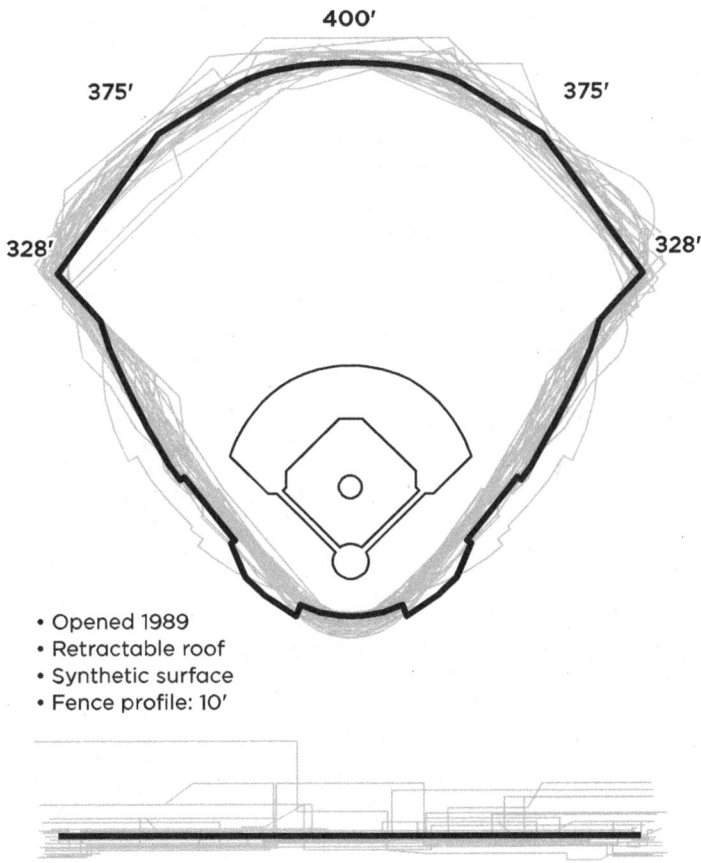

- Opened 1989
- Retractable roof
- Synthetic surface
- Fence profile: 10'

Three-Year Park Factors

Runs	Runs/RH	Runs/LH	HR/RH	HR/LH
102	102	101	102	100

Blue Jays Team Analysis

The one-sided, parasocial interactions that attach us to sports can express themselves in all sorts of ways, especially in baseball where a long season can alter the understanding of a team's chances or motivations dozens of times before the year ends. Usually, that emotional vacillation is tied to on-field performance. For the 2018 Toronto Blue Jays, facing long odds in the hyper-competitive American League East, the focus was weighted far more to members of the organization not on the field in Toronto at all.

The developments providing any sort of parasocial feedback to the brains of those following Canada's only MLB team happened mostly in the minor leagues, with a few occurring off the field. From before last offseason even officially began, when the Blue Jays declined their team option on Jose Bautista, there were signals that there would be little to latch on to at Rogers Centre. Third baseman Josh Donaldson's shoulder problems added to that trend. By the time Donaldson landed on the disabled list in late May, the Jays were 25-29, already 12 games back in the division and in the fourth-place spot they'd hold for the remainder of the season.

Add to that reliever Roberto Osuna being arrested for domestic assault in May and being placed on administrative leave before eventually being suspended 75 games by the league and traded to the Astros at the deadline, and the likelihood of anyone finding emotional satisfaction on the major-league roster was slim. Lost years happen and this was one of them for Toronto. But that's the nice thing about baseball, with its many different levels and hundreds of active players in each organization—there's usually an alternate source of entertainment if the big club is falling on its face.

Which is why the majority of the Jays' narrative in 2018 centered around minor leaguers like Bo Bichette, Danny Jansen, Cavan Biggio and of course Vladimir Guerrero Jr., the 19-year-old phenom who held the spotlight all season as he dominated three levels of the minors by hitting .381/.437/.636. But the constant frustration of the Jays keeping him in the minors despite that success went hand in hand with the enjoyment that came from watching him play (or at least reading the box scores of his games).

Normally the one-sided, parasocial relationships people find in sports stem from a win-loss record of a statistically marvelous season or a race to make history either as an entire roster or as an individual, but the attachment to Vlad Jr. wasn't entirely that type of case. Yes, his on-field prowess was magnetic, yet that attention was undercut by the fact that he never made an appearance in Toronto. Even when there was an obvious opening for the Blue Jays to call him up, they did not, leading to sympathy for Vlad Jr. and questions about the role of service-time suppression in prospect development.

An apt comparison can be found not in sports, but in a major facet of the British Commonwealth of which Canada is a part—the royal family. Specifically, the one-sided relationship royal watchers worldwide have crafted around Prince Harry, Duke of Sussex. Vlad Jr. and Prince Harry—separated by an ocean and an occupation, but connected by the sphere of an adoring public projecting emotions onto them—do not create a perfectly matched metaphor, but the emotional aspect is more alike than not. Both are partially famous due to their father's fame before them and both are succeeding in the face of high expectations out of their control.

It's easy to attach personal hopes onto each of them, and equally easy to be disappointed on their behalf when they can't publicly be dissatisfied with their circumstances or are seemingly kept from the satisfaction others believe they deserve. Harry's life provides a lens through which we can understand the burgeoning attachment to Vlad Jr. and the ways in which he's been locked into a pre-prescribed role for baseball fans, along with how that narrative consumed the Jays' 2018 season more than the team on the field in Toronto.

Harry's status as a canvas on which the public can paint their own desires stems from a mix of his brand of charm and the natural limitations of his public role, and public setbacks he's experienced only exacerbated this projection by observers. This all mimics the current situation with Guerrero and Jays fans. Once that type of psychological attachment is formed it's hard to break, at least until the desired outcome has been achieved. As with any sizable output of emotional resources a positive outcome is the hoped-for result, even if the fans in question may not consciously realize how mentally stimulating that outcome would be.

With Guerrero, the specific setbacks in his path to a suitable level of "happiness" as decided by fans—here, reaching the major leagues—are easily trackable and meted out entirely by the Blue Jays' front office. Guerrero was already a known quantity in baseball before the season began, the weight of the "Jr." in Vlad Jr. If you didn't know of him, he changed that quickly with a home run in a preseason exhibition game at Montreal's Olympic Stadium, the same ballpark in which his father starred.

He became more than just another great prospect by early May, when his mashing of baseballs began to reach levels impossible to be bored by, like when he hit the side of a hotel behind the New Hampshire Fisher Cats field with a homer. So when Donaldson got hurt near the end of that month and the team declined to use that opportunity to call up Guerrero, the public was insulted on his behalf. A week later, with Guerrero hitting .409 at Double-A, the Jays not only declined to call him up once again, but also deferred on even promoting him to Triple-A.

At that point, June 5, the Blue Jays were 26-34 and in fourth place, so all fan focus, outrage and joy was firmly hitched to Guerrero's progress. The Jays cited his defensive shakiness as the primary reason he needed more time in the minors, and the response was a call for them to let him work on his defense in the majors as the team was dead in the water. Their blatant service-time manipulation was more important to them than fan satisfaction. It's a situation we'll see many more times in many more cities before the trend stops. Vlad Jr. remained in the minors to finish the Triple-A season, hitting .336/.414/.564 with six homers in 30 games there. The Blue Jays' season was a failure by any measure and they still refused to provide the second-hand satisfaction so many craved.

As Harry is to his mother, Guerrero emulates some of the most memorable and beloved aspects of his father's personality and career. In his batting stance, in his smile, in his enthusiasm and appreciation for the game. When he injured his knee and went on the disabled list just a few days after this latest short shrift, it elicited the same type of reaction as when Prince Harry got dumped or unfairly overshadowed. How dare they? He deserves better than this. He deserves everything.

What do the fans who're watching him be artificially limited by his employer deserve? The continuing rationalizations from the Jays are some of the least subtle excuses to ever come from a professional sports team, but they are far from the first to resort to this same song and dance to keep a player under their control for an extra season. Service-time manipulation has been a problem for a long time now, but only in recent years (Kris Bryant's public unhappiness with the Cubs in 2014 being a prime example) has the issue gotten so bad that media and fans have begun trying to hold teams accountable. Guerrero has the potential to be the tipping point.

Rooting for a bad team is one thing. Seeing them not make smart decisions to fix performance issues is another. But worst of all is this type of blatant disregard for the team's improvement—actively preventing someone who could make the team better or at least more fun from joining them for the express purpose of keeping the player under their control for a bit longer. Vlad Jr. is such a vibrant, easy-to-root-for person that the manipulation feels that much sharper a betrayal because it's apparent there would be immediate results when adding him to the roster, in both wins and fan morale.

Before this case, intense attachment to young players stopped short of being a net negative for a team manipulating their service time, but as social media and increased access to prospect information allow fan attachment to happen earlier and earlier the downside of teams choosing this strategy becomes more acute.

Toronto Blue Jays 2019

Being angered on Guerrero's behalf is a natural extension of fans finally getting fed up with how teams are dismissing their desires, even if that connection isn't a conscious decision by supporters, but rather a subconscious instinct.

In September, once it was confirmed that Toronto would not be calling up Vlad Jr. even after the minor-league season was over, the MLBPA issued a statement saying, "It's bad for the Blue Jays, it's bad for fans, it's bad for players and it's bad for the industry." But the knitting of fans' emotional uplift to that of a player who hadn't even played for the Toronto crowd could have told you that already. It carried over to the offseason as well, with Guerrero taking cuts or working on his defense eliciting just as emphatic a reaction from the masses. It's now consumed the narrative of the Blue Jays as an organization.

With that more than apparent, the Jays still did not acquiesce to public pressure to call him up. Toronto remained steadfast on their service-time manipulation course despite a groundswell against it. A main facet of parasocial relationships is not just the attachment and interest between the aware subject and the unaware subject, but a loyalty from the former toward the latter. Combine that with the base amount of loyalty present in any fan-team relationship and you get layers of dedication building to increasing unhappiness when that loyalty is insulted.

The Jays are not yet swayed by their fans' dissatisfaction. Whether that's because fans have not yet taken their loyalty elsewhere in large enough numbers for the team to notice, or because that number no longer exists thanks to the many other streams of revenue therefore negating the loyalty completely, is hard to tell just yet. Vlad Jr. being kept down and how the situation resolves itself in 2019 could end up being proof that such intensely focused fan loyalty toward a player is something to which teams actually listen, or proof there's no level of fan attachment that can force owners and front offices to change their business-first approach.

The Jays transformed from a normal baseball team to a conduit through which fans experienced waves of Vladimir Guerrero Jr. news. For a team that looks fated to be stuck behind the same two teams in the division for the foreseeable future, this does not appear to be a situation that will change. If anything, it can only be rectified by giving the masses what they want in Vlad Jr.'s ascendancy. Prince Harry followers finally got a major emotional payoff in 2018. This season, people similarly attached to Guerrero may get the payoff they've wished for as well.

—*Whitney McIntosh is a freelance writer from Brooklyn, NY.*

Part 2: Player Analysis

Toronto Blue Jays 2019

Brandon Drury   UT
Born: 08/21/92   Age: 26   Bats: R   Throws: R
Height: 6'2"   Weight: 210   Origin: Round 13, 2010 Draft (#404 overall)

YEAR	TEAM	LVL	AGE	PA	R	2B	3B	HR	RBI	BB	K	SB	CS	AVG/OBP/SLG
2016	ARI	MLB	23	499	59	31	1	16	53	31	100	1	1	.282/.329/.458
2017	ARI	MLB	24	480	41	37	2	13	63	28	103	1	1	.267/.317/.447
2018	SWB	AAA	25	235	30	13	1	5	30	32	58	3	1	.291/.400/.442
2018	NYA	MLB	25	57	2	2	0	1	7	5	12	0	0	.176/.263/.275
2018	TOR	MLB	25	29	3	2	0	0	3	2	8	0	0	.154/.241/.231
2019	TOR	MLB	26	293	31	15	1	8	34	22	66	1	1	.252/.314/.406

Breakout: 12%   Improve: 57%   Collapse: 6%   Attrition: 19%   MLB: 95%
Comparables: Wilmer Flores, Brent Morel, Matt Duffy

Once a versatile defender known for his sizzling, if streaky, bat, Drury saw his major-league career evaporate quicker than a midsummer heat spell snapped by a Southern Oregon sunset. After switching over to the American League, he labored through the first half of the season with sub-Mendoza Line production levels and saw his stats plummet even further when the Yankees swapped him for Toronto lefty J.A. Happ. That said, it was mostly due to the 93-mph sinker that fractured his left hand just prior to the trade. Now, it's not a matter of whether or not he can bounce back from a career-worst performance, but whether he'll receive ample playing time to return as the quasi-utility player of years past.

YEAR	TEAM	LVL	AGE	PA	DRC+	VORP	BABIP	BRR	FRAA	WARP
2016	ARI	MLB	23	499	98	18.6	.327	1.9	LF(62): -5.2, RF(32): -1.8	0.4
2017	ARI	MLB	24	480	83	10.1	.320	-3.9	2B(114): 2.5, 3B(1): -0.2	0.3
2018	SWB	AAA	25	235	130	19.7	.390	-1.0	3B(45): 2.4, 1B(5): 0.7	1.4
2018	NYA	MLB	25	57	78	-2.1	.211	0.1	3B(9): -0.7, 2B(5): -0.1	-0.1
2018	TOR	MLB	25	29	80	-1.8	.222	0.0	3B(6): -0.1, 2B(2): -0.6	0.0
2019	TOR	MLB	26	293	93	6.7	.307	-0.6	2B 1, 3B -1	0.6

Brandon Drury, continued

Batted Ball Distribution

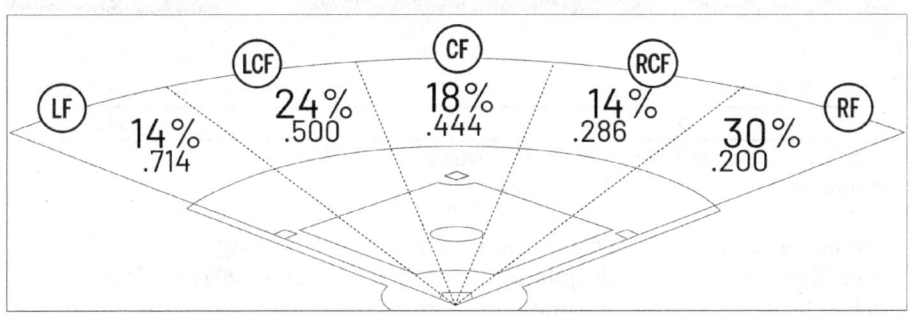

Strike Zone vs LHP

Strike Zone vs RHP

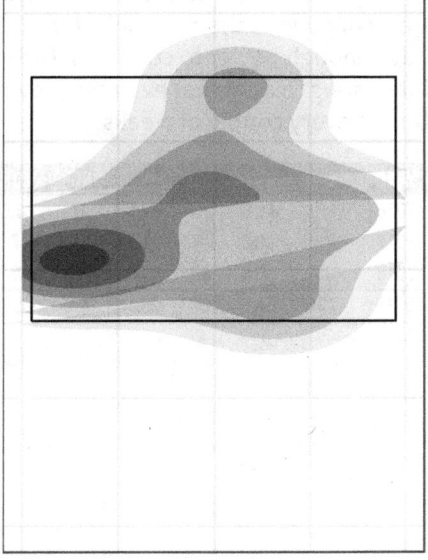

Freddy Galvis SS

Born: 11/14/89   Age: 29   Bats: B   Throws: R
Height: 5'10"   Weight: 185   Origin: International Free Agent, 2006

YEAR	TEAM	LVL	AGE	PA	R	2B	3B	HR	RBI	BB	K	SB	CS	AVG/OBP/SLG
2016	PHI	MLB	26	624	61	26	3	20	67	25	136	17	6	.241/.274/.399
2017	PHI	MLB	27	663	71	29	6	12	61	45	111	14	5	.255/.309/.382
2018	SDN	MLB	28	656	62	31	5	13	67	45	147	8	6	.248/.299/.380
2019	TOR	MLB	29	262	28	13	2	6	28	17	53	5	2	.254/.307/.400

Breakout: 7%   Improve: 52%   Collapse: 7%   Attrition: 12%   MLB: 94%
Comparables: Adam Everett, Jack Wilson, Rich Aurilia

Coming up, Galvis was the classic punchless but slick-fielding shortstop (and he's still very good there, despite what FRAA thought of his 2018 performance). Each of his early BP annual comments features some variation of that analysis, best encapsulated by Kevin Goldstein in 2012: "When discussing Galvis's hitting, it's worth noting that he has an excellent glove." But a funny thing happened when the league rolled out a new ball. Once anemic, Galvis's bat suddenly had 20-homer pop, and in 2018 he reached double-digits for the third year running. He's not *good* at the dish: he's still a .250 hitter who rarely walks and he doesn't have enough power to compensate for the first two problems. It's nonetheless interesting to note that even the glove-first shortstops in 2018 can run into a homer every couple of weeks.

YEAR	TEAM	LVL	AGE	PA	DRC+	VORP	BABIP	BRR	FRAA	WARP
2016	PHI	MLB	26	624	77	8.6	.280	-3.5	SS(156): 0.5	0.7
2017	PHI	MLB	27	663	85	27.3	.292	1.6	SS(155): 1.7, CF(1): 0.1	2.2
2018	SDN	MLB	28	656	82	18.5	.304	-1.2	SS(160): -8.9, 2B(5): -0.5	0.4
2019	TOR	MLB	29	262	87	6.2	.297	0.1	SS -1	0.5

Freddy Galvis, continued

Batted Ball Distribution

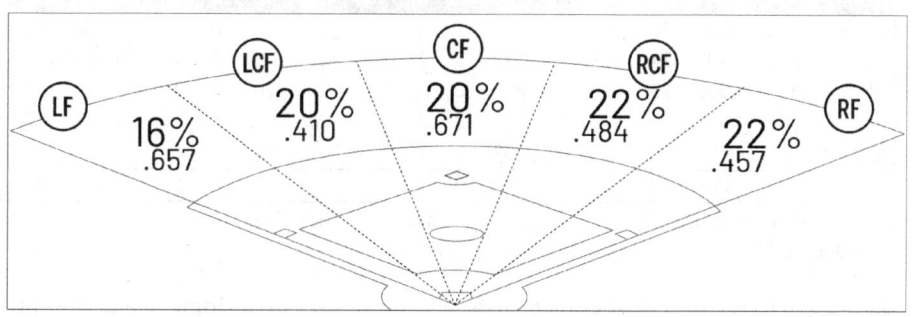

Strike Zone vs LHP   **Strike Zone vs RHP**

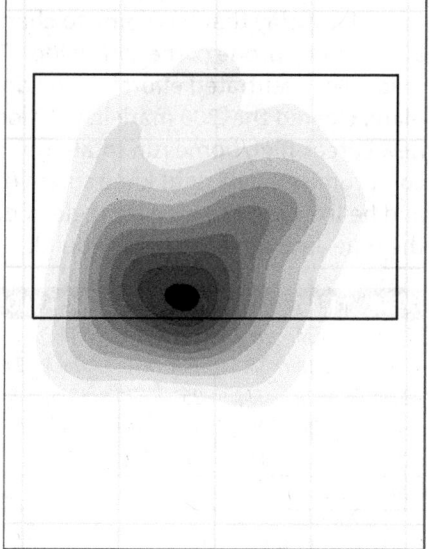

Toronto Blue Jays 2019

Randal Grichuk OF

Born: 08/13/91   Age: 27   Bats: R   Throws: R
Height: 6'1"   Weight: 205   Origin: Round 1, 2009 Draft (#24 overall)

YEAR	TEAM	LVL	AGE	PA	R	2B	3B	HR	RBI	BB	K	SB	CS	AVG/OBP/SLG
2016	MEM	AAA	24	86	12	4	1	6	18	2	14	0	0	.272/.302/.568
2016	SLN	MLB	24	478	66	29	3	24	68	28	141	5	4	.240/.289/.480
2017	MEM	AAA	25	67	11	3	0	6	9	3	20	0	0	.270/.313/.603
2017	SLN	MLB	25	442	53	25	3	22	59	26	133	6	1	.238/.285/.473
2018	TOR	MLB	26	462	60	32	1	25	61	27	122	3	2	.245/.301/.502
2019	TOR	MLB	27	497	63	27	2	23	67	34	134	5	2	.246/.304/.465

Breakout: 10%   Improve: 51%   Collapse: 9%   Attrition: 8%   MLB: 90%
Comparables: Mark Trumbo, Oswaldo Arcia, Corey Dickerson

If we were to condense Grichuk's professional career into a single event, it might look something like the gruesome aftermath of a Brandon Guyer foul ball on September 9. Grichuk hightailed it from right field, kicked out his feet for a slide, and was promptly decked by the business end of a security guard's stool. While he escaped with nothing more serious than facial bruising, it was the kind of all-or-nothing play that has come to characterize his playing style as a speedy, albeit injury-prone corner outfielder. That's not to say 2018 was a total bust—he made a concentrated effort to tone down his swing-happy approach at the plate, cleared the .300 mark in OBP for the first time in years and worked up to a new career-high home run total—but his availability was once again compromised by a right knee sprain (the result of another catch gone wrong), and he'll enter 2019 with a gaggle of outfield prospects nipping at his heels as the Blue Jays advance their rebuild.

YEAR	TEAM	LVL	AGE	PA	DRC+	VORP	BABIP	BRR	FRAA	WARP
2016	MEM	AAA	24	86	114	6.4	.258	0.4	CF(17): -0.2	0.3
2016	SLN	MLB	24	478	96	24.0	.294	2.2	CF(115): 0.6, LF(4): 0.6	1.7
2017	MEM	AAA	25	67	125	5.0	.297	0.0	LF(9): 3.6, CF(1): -0.1	0.6
2017	SLN	MLB	25	442	95	11.4	.293	1.9	LF(58): -2.7, RF(55): 4.8	1.2
2018	TOR	MLB	26	462	109	19.5	.282	2.5	RF(102): 2.4, CF(26): -2.3	1.9
2019	TOR	MLB	27	497	100	16.3	.293	-0.4	RF 5	1.7

Randal Grichuk, continued

Batted Ball Distribution

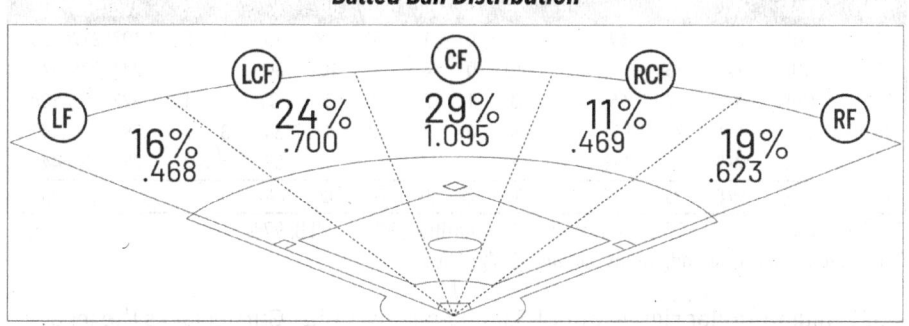

Strike Zone vs LHP **Strike Zone vs RHP**

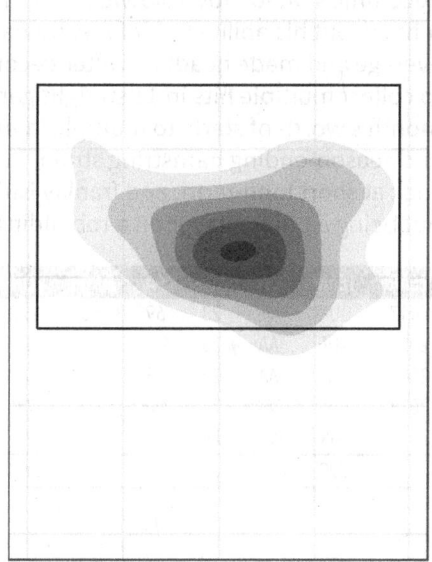

Toronto Blue Jays 2019

Lourdes Gurriel MI
Born: 10/10/93 Age: 25 Bats: R Throws: R
Height: 6'2" Weight: 185 Origin: International Free Agent, 2016

YEAR	TEAM	LVL	AGE	PA	R	2B	3B	HR	RBI	BB	K	SB	CS	AVG/OBP/SLG
2017	DUN	A+	23	69	6	1	0	1	8	2	13	1	0	.197/.217/.258
2017	NHP	AA	23	185	20	10	0	4	28	10	30	2	0	.241/.286/.371
2018	NHP	AA	24	65	7	3	1	2	14	3	8	1	1	.322/.354/.508
2018	BUF	AAA	24	156	20	8	0	5	30	4	34	3	2	.293/.321/.449
2018	TOR	MLB	24	263	30	8	0	11	35	9	59	1	2	.281/.309/.446
2019	TOR	MLB	25	661	85	30	2	23	76	32	146	5	3	.268/.309/.435

Breakout: 9% Improve: 57% Collapse: 12% Attrition: 33% MLB: 97%
Comparables: Ian Desmond, Danny Santana, Josh Rutledge

A $22 million-dollar signee out of Sancti Spiritus, Cuba, Gurriel lacks the legacy of his father, Lourdes Sr., and the established star status of his brother, Yulieski. Neither of those facts overshadowed his first foray into major-league ball, though, where he proved a surprisingly capable alternative to a decommissioned Troy Tulowitzki in 2018. Gurriel's approach isn't exactly refined, but his ability to hit for extra bases brought him to the cusp of a .300 average and made headlines after becoming second player in the last 50 years to collect multiple hits in 11 straight games. The downside? He lost nearly a month's worth of starts to multiple injuries, including a concussion, ankle sprain and season-ending hamstring strain. Even when healthy, he lacks the glove to stick at short long-term, and frankly isn't likely to be above-average anywhere, but being a utility player on a rebuilding team has its benefits.

YEAR	TEAM	LVL	AGE	PA	DRC+	VORP	BABIP	BRR	FRAA	WARP
2017	DUN	A+	23	69	63	-3.2	.226	0.3	SS(11): -0.2, 2B(1): 0.1	-0.2
2017	NHP	AA	23	185	74	4.2	.266	1.2	2B(22): 1.5, SS(17): 0.9	0.1
2018	NHP	AA	24	65	130	6.7	.333	0.3	2B(7): -0.1, SS(5): -0.7	0.3
2018	BUF	AAA	24	156	116	7.0	.345	-0.9	SS(23): 0.9, 2B(9): 0.2	0.7
2018	TOR	MLB	24	263	104	9.0	.326	-1.7	SS(46): -0.8, 2B(24): -1.1	0.8
2019	TOR	MLB	25	661	95	20.1	.312	-1.1	SS -1, 2B 3	2.1

Lourdes Gurriel, continued

Batted Ball Distribution

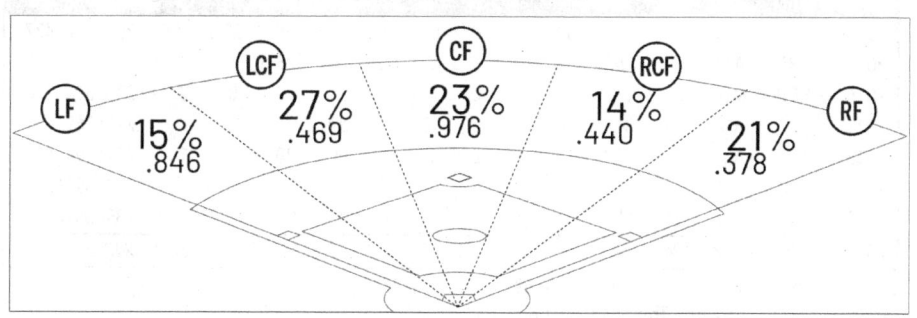

Strike Zone vs LHP   **Strike Zone vs RHP**

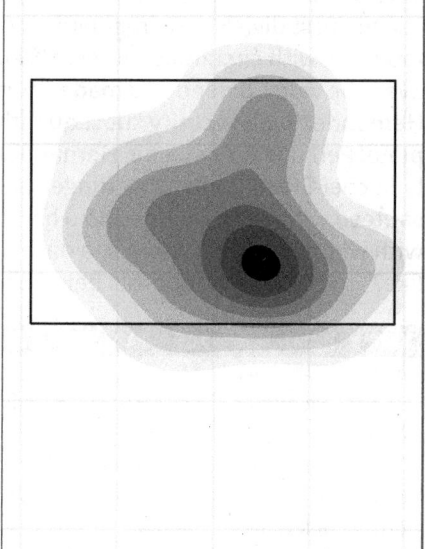

Teoscar Hernandez OF

Born: 10/15/92 Age: 26 Bats: R Throws: R
Height: 6'2" Weight: 180 Origin: International Free Agent, 2011

YEAR	TEAM	LVL	AGE	PA	R	2B	3B	HR	RBI	BB	K	SB	CS	AVG/OBP/SLG
2016	CCH	AA	23	322	53	19	0	6	30	32	55	29	11	.305/.384/.437
2016	FRE	AAA	23	160	20	9	3	4	23	13	25	5	4	.313/.365/.500
2016	HOU	MLB	23	112	15	7	0	4	11	11	28	0	2	.230/.304/.420
2017	FRE	AAA	24	347	54	20	3	12	44	39	72	12	7	.279/.369/.485
2017	BUF	AAA	24	109	14	6	2	6	22	8	30	4	1	.222/.294/.505
2017	TOR	MLB	24	95	16	6	0	8	20	6	36	0	1	.261/.305/.602
2018	TOR	MLB	25	523	67	29	7	22	57	41	163	5	5	.239/.302/.468
2019	TOR	MLB	26	398	56	20	4	15	46	33	107	9	5	.248/.315/.451

Breakout: 7%   Improve: 45%   Collapse: 9%   Attrition: 18%   MLB: 86%
Comparables: Eric Thames, Trey Mancini, Corey Dickerson

No matter how you slice it—and when it comes to the metaphorical pie of player value, there are a lot of ways to slice it—Hernandez was the Blue Jays' worst defender and one of the most poorly-graded outfielders to grace the American League East division. He regularly dodged routine fly balls and paired clunky footwork with circuitous routes, off-kilter instincts and poor communication. Even the worst defender is made valuable by virtue of a hot bat, however, and Hernandez's job security subsequently took the form of a masterful swing at the plate. Perhaps it's not a pie Hernandez resembles after all, but an English trifle a la Rachel Green: tantalizing dinger-laced ladyfingers at the bottom, ground beef sauteed with peas, onions and a handful of fielding errors in the center, topped with whipped cream and just a dash of unfounded optimism. "What's not to like?" the Blue Jays mumble between forkfuls.

YEAR	TEAM	LVL	AGE	PA	DRC+	VORP	BABIP	BRR	FRAA	WARP
2016	CCH	AA	23	322	143	25.6	.359	4.2	RF(37): -1.2, CF(30): -0.6	1.9
2016	FRE	AAA	23	160	125	8.7	.350	-2.4	RF(26): 4.1, CF(11): -1.8	0.5
2016	HOU	MLB	23	112	91	0.6	.275	-0.6	LF(22): -1.5, CF(15): -1.3	-0.2
2017	FRE	AAA	24	347	124	21.7	.329	1.9	RF(44): 2.2, CF(22): 1.4	1.9
2017	BUF	AAA	24	109	99	4.9	.254	0.8	RF(10): 0.8, CF(7): 1.0	0.7
2017	TOR	MLB	24	95	101	8.4	.333	1.9	LF(18): -0.7, CF(5): 0.0	0.4
2018	TOR	MLB	25	523	104	12.8	.313	-0.1	LF(87): -2.0, RF(35): 0.7	1.3
2019	TOR	MLB	26	398	99	11.5	.305	0.0	LF -1, RF 2	1.1

Teoscar Hernandez, continued

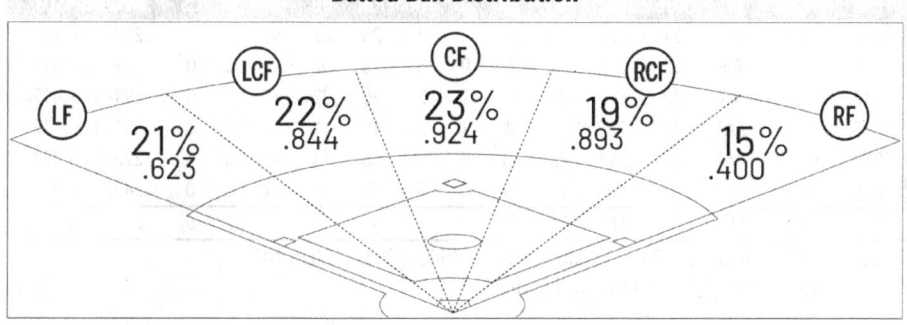

Batted Ball Distribution

Strike Zone vs LHP   **Strike Zone vs RHP**

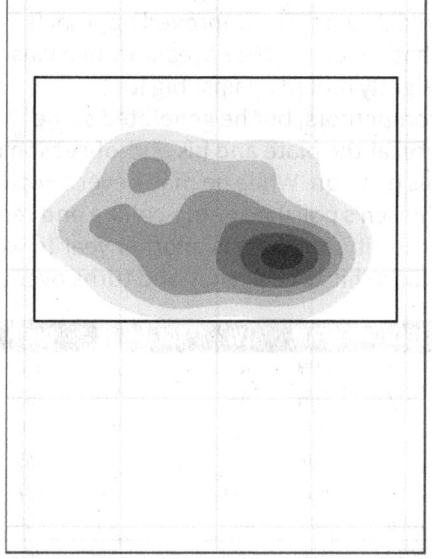

Toronto Blue Jays 2019

Danny Jansen C
Born: 04/15/95   Age: 24   Bats: R   Throws: R
Height: 6'2"   Weight: 225   Origin: Round 16, 2013 Draft (#475 overall)

YEAR	TEAM	LVL	AGE	PA	R	2B	3B	HR	RBI	BB	K	SB	CS	AVG/OBP/SLG
2016	DUN	A+	21	217	18	7	0	1	23	22	40	7	1	.218/.313/.271
2017	DUN	A+	22	136	19	6	0	5	18	8	14	0	0	.369/.422/.541
2017	NHP	AA	22	210	23	15	1	2	20	22	19	1	0	.291/.378/.419
2017	BUF	AAA	22	78	8	4	1	3	10	11	7	0	0	.328/.423/.552
2018	BUF	AAA	23	360	45	21	1	12	58	44	49	5	1	.275/.390/.473
2018	TOR	MLB	23	95	12	6	0	3	8	9	17	0	0	.247/.347/.432
2019	TOR	MLB	24	412	50	18	1	14	48	42	77	2	0	.235/.330/.409

Breakout: 12%   Improve: 39%   Collapse: 7%   Attrition: 23%   MLB: 74%
Comparables: Josh Bell, Conor Jackson, J.R. Towles

The heir apparent to incumbent backstop Russell Martin, Jansen was tasked with his first major league workload after getting called up in mid-August. The improved approach that fueled his 2017 breakthrough was slightly muted against big league competitors, but he generated some pop at the plate and his end-of-season numbers still skewed above average for his position. While he may never become a true fixture in the heart of the lineup, Jansen's polished game-calling and receiving skills give him a deserved air of maturity, and he has another year to work as an apprentice before Russell Martin hits free agency and turns over the keys to the gear.

YEAR	TEAM	P. COUNT	FRM RUNS	BLK RUNS	THRW RUNS	TOT RUNS
2017	BUF	2610	0.0	0.1	-0.1	0.2
2017	NHP	6546	-2.1	2.2	0.0	-0.8
2018	BUF	7393	-4.6	0.2	-0.1	-4.0
2018	TOR	3560	0.6	0.7	-0.2	1.8
2019	TOR	15689	-8.5	1.9	-1.8	-8.4

YEAR	TEAM	LVL	AGE	PA	DRC+	VORP	BABIP	BRR	FRAA	WARP
2016	DUN	A+	21	217	84	0.6	.268	-0.2	C(50): -1.3	0.0
2017	DUN	A+	22	136	183	17.1	.385	-0.7	C(25): -2.0	1.1
2017	NHP	AA	22	210	119	15.5	.311	-1.4	C(52): -0.9	0.8
2017	BUF	AAA	22	78	165	11.2	.333	-0.1	C(21): -0.4	0.7
2018	BUF	AAA	23	360	137	32.9	.292	0.2	C(56): -6.0	1.7
2018	TOR	MLB	23	95	100	6.6	.274	0.9	C(29): 1.0	0.7
2019	TOR	MLB	24	412	99	18.4	.262	-0.6	C -12	0.5

Danny Jansen, *continued*

Batted Ball Distribution

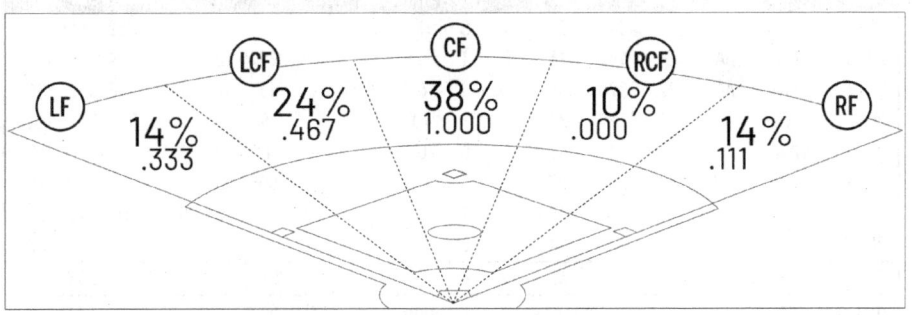

Strike Zone vs LHP **Strike Zone vs RHP**

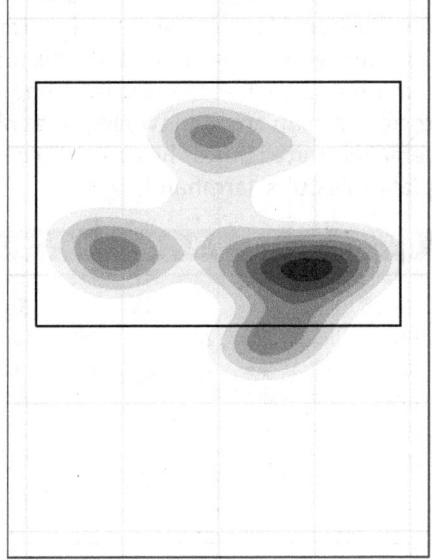

Toronto Blue Jays 2019

Billy McKinney OF
Born: 08/23/94 Age: 24 Bats: L Throws: L
Height: 6'1" Weight: 205 Origin: Round 1, 2013 Draft (#24 overall)

YEAR	TEAM	LVL	AGE	PA	R	2B	3B	HR	RBI	BB	K	SB	CS	AVG/OBP/SLG
2016	TEN	AA	21	349	37	12	3	1	31	47	68	2	4	.252/.355/.322
2016	TRN	AA	21	142	15	7	1	3	13	12	29	2	2	.234/.310/.375
2017	TRN	AA	22	276	34	16	4	6	29	30	45	2	1	.250/.339/.431
2017	SWB	AAA	22	224	32	13	3	10	35	9	49	0	0	.306/.336/.541
2018	NYA	MLB	23	4	0	0	0	0	0	0	1	0	0	.250/.250/.250
2018	SWB	AAA	23	234	27	8	5	13	32	21	56	0	0	.226/.299/.495
2018	BUF	AAA	23	72	10	3	2	3	8	8	16	0	0	.203/.292/.453
2018	TOR	MLB	23	128	14	7	0	6	13	11	32	1	0	.252/.320/.470
2019	TOR	MLB	24	476	58	22	4	19	56	32	120	1	1	.225/.283/.425

Breakout: 12%   Improve: 34%   Collapse: 5%   Attrition: 28%   MLB: 55%
Comparables: Kole Calhoun, Moises Sierra, Shin-Soo Choo

Ever the man on the move, McKinney ricocheted around the league as an almost featured piece in several blockbuster trades over the last few years. After a deadline deal for J.A. Happ was finalized last summer, he finally settled down in Toronto, where he slurped down his first cup of coffee in the majors with a mature approach at the plate and enough power to buoy his spot on the active roster. With an arm and two legs that play only in left field, however, his utility remains limited unless he can rediscover some of that promise he showed at the plate as a Cubs' farmhand.

YEAR	TEAM	LVL	AGE	PA	DRC+	VORP	BABIP	BRR	FRAA	WARP
2016	TEN	AA	21	349	115	5.4	.320	-0.1	RF(74): 0.0, LF(3): 1.1	0.6
2016	TRN	AA	21	142	106	3.5	.281	-0.8	RF(32): 1.4, CF(1): 0.2	0.2
2017	TRN	AA	22	276	104	13.5	.277	0.3	RF(50): 12.3, LF(10): -1.1	1.6
2017	SWB	AAA	22	224	124	13.0	.353	-0.7	RF(26): 1.6, LF(26): 0.1	0.8
2018	NYA	MLB	23	4	98	-0.1	.333	0.0	LF(2): -0.2	0.0
2018	SWB	AAA	23	234	99	7.6	.245	0.5	RF(32): -1.8, CF(12): 1.6	0.1
2018	BUF	AAA	23	72	103	0.9	.222	0.4	RF(14): 3.3, 1B(4): 0.0	0.4
2018	TOR	MLB	23	128	99	2.9	.295	-1.9	LF(26): -0.3, RF(13): -0.3	0.0
2019	TOR	MLB	24	476	83	4.7	.262	-0.5	LF -4	-0.1

Billy McKinney, continued

Batted Ball Distribution

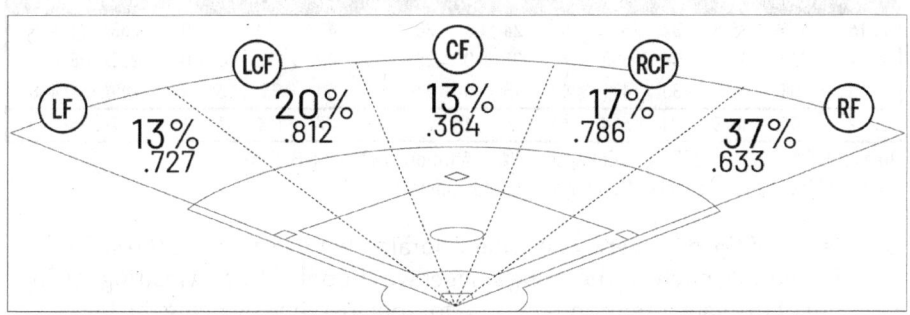

Strike Zone vs LHP **Strike Zone vs RHP**

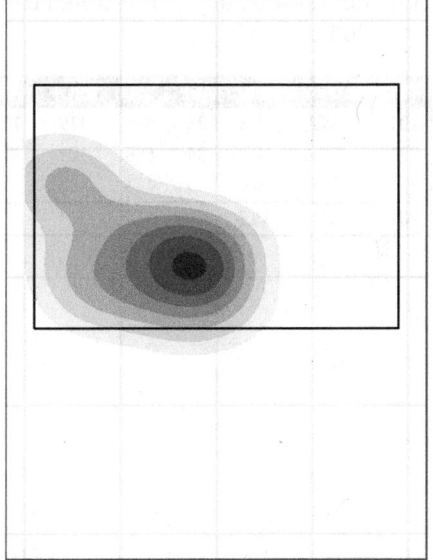

Kendrys Morales DH

Born: 06/20/83   Age: 36   Bats: B   Throws: R
Height: 6'1"   Weight: 225   Origin: International Free Agent, 2005

YEAR	TEAM	LVL	AGE	PA	R	2B	3B	HR	RBI	BB	K	SB	CS	AVG/OBP/SLG
2016	KCA	MLB	33	618	65	24	0	30	93	48	120	0	0	.263/.327/.468
2017	TOR	MLB	34	608	67	25	0	28	85	43	132	0	0	.250/.308/.445
2018	TOR	MLB	35	471	47	15	0	21	57	50	95	2	3	.249/.331/.438
2019	TOR	MLB	36	554	65	26	1	21	73	47	114	1	1	.257/.325/.440

Breakout: 0%   Improve: 20%   Collapse: 24%   Attrition: 18%   MLB: 82%
Comparables: Adrian Gonzalez, Don Baylor, Harold Baines

God help us if the day ever comes when Morales' bat fails to parse the strike zone for hittable pitches. The aging slugger was hobbled by a hamstring strain right out of the gate, then compensated for that lost time by being the best overall hitter on the Jays by DRC+. The only thing more intriguing than his seven-game home run tear through the AL and NL East—a streak that put him in the esteemed company of former major leaguers Kevin Mench, Barry Bonds and Jim Thome—was the pair of stolen bases he managed to nab, including his first since 2009.

YEAR	TEAM	LVL	AGE	PA	DRC+	VORP	BABIP	BRR	FRAA	WARP
2016	KCA	MLB	33	618	119	11.7	.283	-1.2	1B(7): -0.1, RF(5): -0.2	2.1
2017	TOR	MLB	34	608	101	-3.6	.278	-6.3	1B(12): -1.3	0.2
2018	TOR	MLB	35	471	112	2.6	.272	-4.1	1B(18): 1.8, P(1): 0.0	1.2
2019	TOR	MLB	36	554	104	9.2	.293	-1.1	1B -1	1.2

Kendrys Morales, continued

Batted Ball Distribution

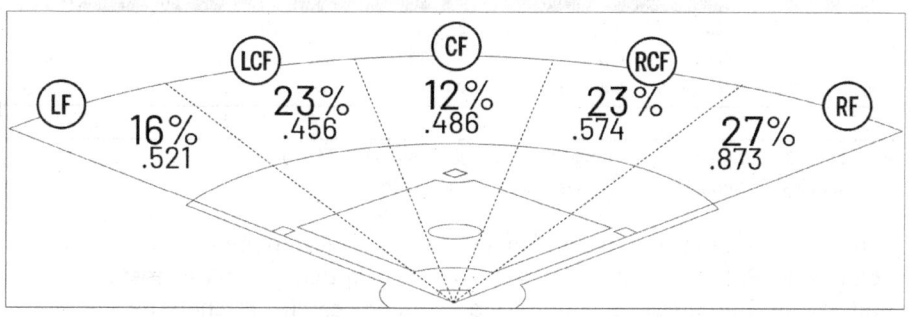

Strike Zone vs LHP   Strike Zone vs RHP

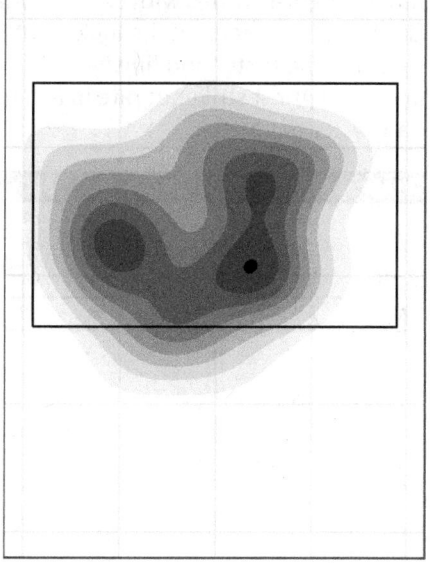

Toronto Blue Jays 2019

Kevin Pillar CF
Born: 01/04/89   Age: 30   Bats: R   Throws: R
Height: 6'0"   Weight: 205   Origin: Round 32, 2011 Draft (#979 overall)

YEAR	TEAM	LVL	AGE	PA	R	2B	3B	HR	RBI	BB	K	SB	CS	AVG/OBP/SLG
2016	TOR	MLB	27	584	59	35	2	7	53	24	90	14	6	.266/.303/.376
2017	TOR	MLB	28	632	72	37	1	16	42	33	95	15	6	.256/.300/.404
2018	TOR	MLB	29	542	65	40	2	15	59	18	98	14	3	.252/.282/.426
2019	TOR	MLB	30	574	64	32	2	14	63	33	96	16	5	.259/.308/.406

Breakout: 5%   Improve: 46%   Collapse: 10%   Attrition: 6%   MLB: 94%
Comparables: Cameron Maybin, Leonys Martin, Angel Pagan

You know what they say: It's all fun and games until someone dislocates their collarbone. Pillar's rough-and-tumble defense landed him in the hospital halfway through the season after a violent diving catch stretched the ligaments in his sternoclavicular joint capsule. It could have been a fatal mishap for the outfielder had the ligaments bent in another direction, but as fortune would have it, he escaped relatively unscathed and was back in uniform by early August. Near-brushes with catastrophe often inspire fervent, if short-lived change in the hearts of the lucky, but Pillar exercised little restraint upon his return to the roster and finished the year with a top-seven FRAA at his position and the highest strikeout rate in any full-season performance of his career to date.

YEAR	TEAM	LVL	AGE	PA	DRC+	VORP	BABIP	BRR	FRAA	WARP
2016	TOR	MLB	27	584	81	4.2	.306	2.7	CF(146): 6.1	1.5
2017	TOR	MLB	28	632	87	7.5	.280	-1.1	CF(153): -6.2	0.5
2018	TOR	MLB	29	542	94	16.5	.281	3.3	CF(142): 9.0	2.8
2019	TOR	MLB	30	574	88	16.1	.291	1.1	CF -2	1.2

Kevin Pillar, continued

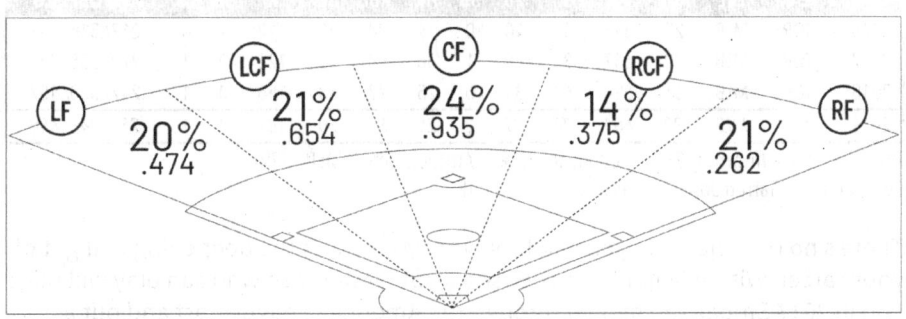

Batted Ball Distribution

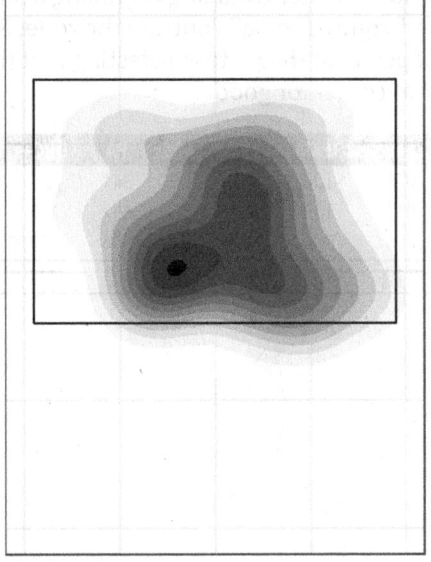

Strike Zone vs LHP   **Strike Zone vs RHP**

Justin Smoak 1B

Born: 12/05/86   Age: 32   Bats: B   Throws: L
Height: 6'4"   Weight: 220   Origin: Round 1, 2008 Draft (#11 overall)

YEAR	TEAM	LVL	AGE	PA	R	2B	3B	HR	RBI	BB	K	SB	CS	AVG/OBP/SLG
2016	TOR	MLB	29	341	33	10	0	14	34	40	112	1	0	.217/.314/.391
2017	TOR	MLB	30	637	85	29	1	38	90	73	128	0	1	.270/.355/.529
2018	TOR	MLB	31	594	67	34	0	25	77	83	156	0	1	.242/.350/.457
2019	TOR	MLB	32	601	74	29	2	25	83	70	147	1	1	.252/.343/.458

Breakout: 0%   Improve: 29%   Collapse: 15%   Attrition: 5%   MLB: 89%
Comparables: Garrett Jones, Lucas Duda, Adam Lind

There's no rule that says you can't reinvent yourself in the deepening twilight of your career. Within Major League Baseball, at least, those who can play will play, and in 2017 Smoak ran ragged through the American League East and put a lusterless lifetime batting line to shame. No crystal ball was needed to foretell the slugger's inevitable regression in 2018—accelerated as it was by a career-worst strikeout rate—but the changes he made during his breakout campaign held fast. After tweaking his timing against offspeed pitches and exercising some self-control on balls outside the zone, Smoak was rewarded with another burst of power at the plate, suggesting that the once-elite prospect may have turned that corner for good.

YEAR	TEAM	LVL	AGE	PA	DRC+	VORP	BABIP	BRR	FRAA	WARP
2016	TOR	MLB	29	341	91	-3.8	.295	-1.3	1B(111): -2.3	-0.3
2017	TOR	MLB	30	637	135	26.6	.285	0.6	1B(151): -0.9	3.6
2018	TOR	MLB	31	594	117	15.1	.297	-5.1	1B(134): -7.2	0.8
2019	TOR	MLB	32	601	114	20.7	.302	-1.3	1B -5	1.6

Justin Smoak, continued

Batted Ball Distribution

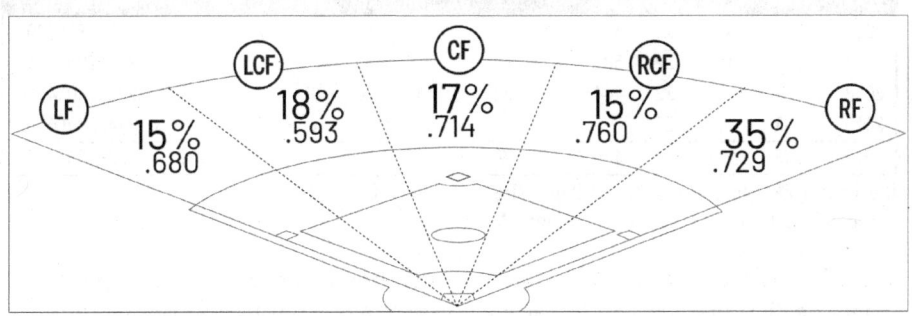

Strike Zone vs LHP   **Strike Zone vs RHP**

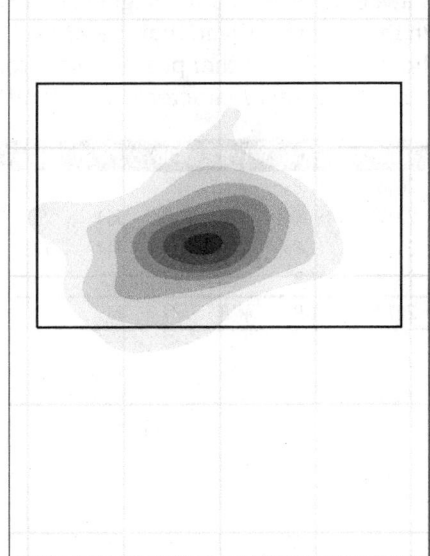

Toronto Blue Jays 2019

Rowdy Tellez   1B
Born: 03/16/95   Age: 24   Bats: L   Throws: L
Height: 6'4"   Weight: 220   Origin: Round 30, 2013 Draft (#895 overall)

YEAR	TEAM	LVL	AGE	PA	R	2B	3B	HR	RBI	BB	K	SB	CS	AVG/OBP/SLG
2016	NHP	AA	21	514	71	29	2	23	81	63	92	4	3	.297/.387/.530
2017	BUF	AAA	22	501	45	29	1	6	56	47	94	6	1	.222/.295/.333
2018	BUF	AAA	23	444	43	22	0	13	50	40	74	7	4	.270/.340/.425
2018	TOR	MLB	23	73	10	9	0	4	14	2	21	0	0	.314/.329/.614
2019	TOR	MLB	24	169	17	9	0	5	19	13	37	1	0	.222/.286/.379

Breakout: 10%   Improve: 38%   Collapse: 1%   Attrition: 30%   MLB: 52%
Comparables: Chris Parmelee, Yonder Alonso, Mike Carp

Tellez finally grew into his name after a much-needed resurgence in Triple-A, where he disrupted his career batting line with a boisterous .298 BABIP and more helium in his swing than you'd find at any local Party City. He got the call to The Show toward the end of the regular season and impressed there, too. That said, his arm and run tool sit near the low end of the 20-80 scale and his flawed plate mechanics suggest that his burst of power may not be sustainable in the long run. Given that the 23-year-old weathered more than most his age, however—his mother passed away from Stage 4 melanoma two weeks prior to his call-up—his character is just about near 80-grade.

YEAR	TEAM	LVL	AGE	PA	DRC+	VORP	BABIP	BRR	FRAA	WARP
2016	NHP	AA	21	514	142	29.7	.324	-0.9	1B(101): -4.9	1.2
2017	BUF	AAA	22	501	80	-11.6	.264	-0.6	1B(115): 1.8	-1.0
2018	BUF	AAA	23	444	123	9.5	.298	-0.8	1B(107): -3.0	0.6
2018	TOR	MLB	23	73	101	5.4	.391	-0.1	1B(17): -0.4	0.1
2019	TOR	MLB	24	169	76	-2.0	.259	-0.3	1B -1	-0.3

Rowdy Tellez, continued

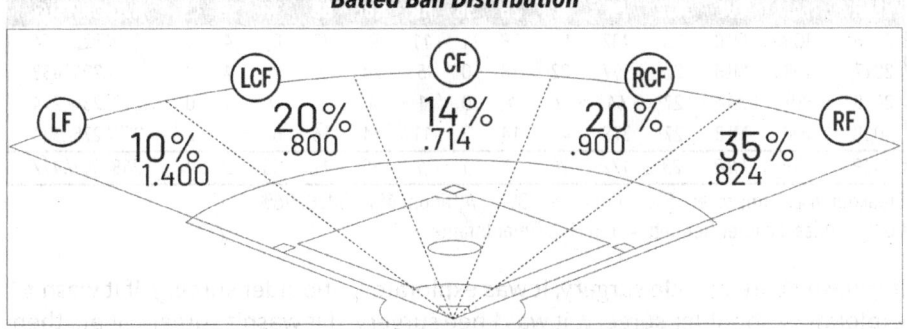

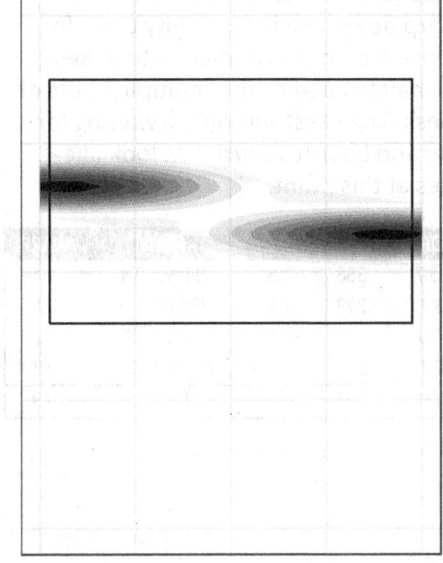

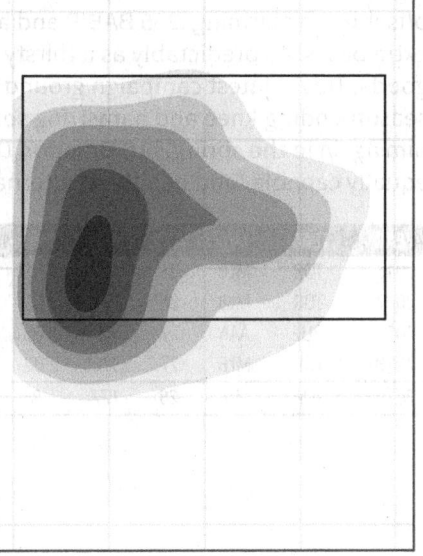

Devon Travis 2B

Born: 02/21/91   Age: 28   Bats: R   Throws: R
Height: 5'9"   Weight: 190   Origin: Round 13, 2012 Draft (#424 overall)

YEAR	TEAM	LVL	AGE	PA	R	2B	3B	HR	RBI	BB	K	SB	CS	AVG/OBP/SLG
2016	TOR	MLB	25	432	54	28	1	11	50	20	87	4	1	.300/.332/.454
2017	TOR	MLB	26	197	22	18	0	5	24	7	38	4	2	.259/.291/.438
2018	BUF	AAA	27	64	9	1	0	1	4	2	7	1	0	.210/.234/.274
2018	TOR	MLB	27	378	41	14	3	11	44	16	64	3	2	.232/.275/.381
2019	TOR	MLB	28	177	20	9	1	5	20	11	33	2	1	.258/.311/.417

Breakout: 4%   Improve: 55%   Collapse: 13%   Attrition: 4%   MLB: 96%
Comparables: Scooter Gennett, Aaron Hill, Omar Infante

If it wasn't core muscle surgery, it was exploratory shoulder surgery. If it wasn't exploratory shoulder surgery, it was knee surgery. If it wasn't surgery at all, then it was an inexplicable decline over his first healthy stretch of pro ball in half a decade. In 2018, Travis' head-scratching results at the plate read like a dour parody of *If You Give a Mouse a Cookie*; though injury-free once more, his career-high 11 home runs and marginally improved walk and strikeout rates were offset by an alarming .255 BABIP and a sharp downturn in his ability to hit for extra bases. As predictably as a thirsty mouse feeding his addiction to baked goods, Travis' latest campaign ground to a halt yet again with multiple bouts of season-ending knee and hamstring soreness. The keystone will be waiting for him again in the spring, but Brandon Drury and Lourdes Gurriel Jr. look like equally capable (and healthier) alternatives at this point.

YEAR	TEAM	LVL	AGE	PA	DRC+	VORP	BABIP	BRR	FRAA	WARP
2016	TOR	MLB	25	432	101	15.7	.358	1.6	2B(99): -0.4	1.4
2017	TOR	MLB	26	197	83	3.4	.299	1.2	2B(50): -1.9	0.1
2018	BUF	AAA	27	64	65	-3.9	.222	0.5	2B(12): 3.1	0.2
2018	TOR	MLB	27	378	82	0.1	.255	0.8	2B(101): -1.5	0.3
2019	TOR	MLB	28	177	86	4.0	.291	-0.1	2B 0	0.3

Devon Travis, continued

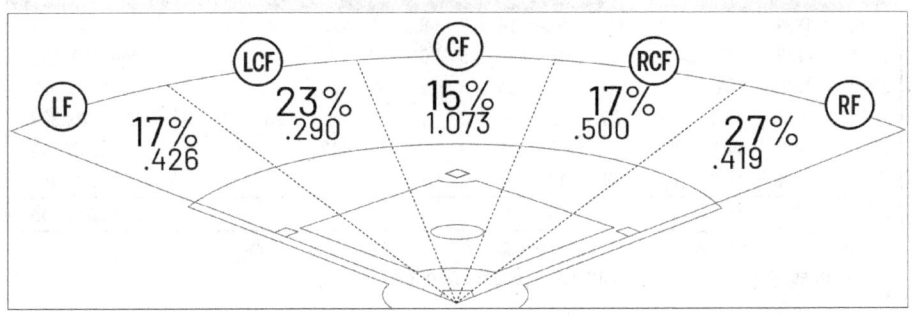

Strike Zone vs LHP   **Strike Zone vs RHP**

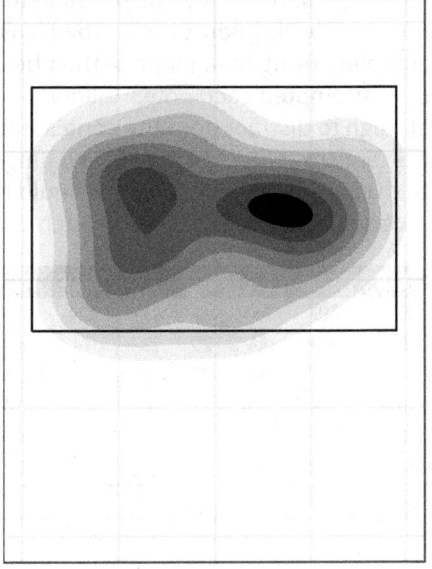

Blue Jays Player Analysis - 41

Richard Urena   MI

Born: 02/26/96   Age: 23   Bats: B   Throws: R
Height: 6'0"   Weight: 185   Origin: International Free Agent, 2012

YEAR	TEAM	LVL	AGE	PA	R	2B	3B	HR	RBI	BB	K	SB	CS	AVG/OBP/SLG
2016	DUN	A+	20	431	52	18	7	8	41	25	64	9	6	.305/.351/.447
2016	NHP	AA	20	132	14	6	5	0	18	4	19	0	2	.266/.282/.395
2017	NHP	AA	21	551	44	36	3	5	60	30	100	0	1	.247/.286/.359
2017	TOR	MLB	21	75	6	4	0	1	4	6	28	1	0	.206/.270/.309
2018	BUF	AAA	22	268	28	11	3	5	29	12	48	2	3	.216/.250/.344
2018	TOR	MLB	22	108	10	4	0	1	6	7	32	2	1	.293/.340/.364
2019	TOR	MLB	23	145	14	6	1	4	15	8	35	1	1	.216/.264/.366

Breakout: 30%   Improve: 40%   Collapse: 6%   Attrition: 31%   MLB: 50%
Comparables: Ronny Cedeno, Christian Arroyo, Jose Rondon

It's difficult to judge a singing competition inasmuch as it's difficult to tell hundreds of people—live, on national television—that the thing they love most in life is the thing for which they have no remarkable talent. In the age of chunky highlights and Britney Spears wannabes, *American Idol* judge Paula Abdul had a knack for letting contestants down easy. "You're so pretty," she'd gush before complimenting their smile or their bedazzled outfit or the passion with which they attempted each note. Hollow though the praise may have been, it was just enough to distract from the contestants' off-key warbling and botched lyrics and the tactless remarks of her fellow judges. Well, Urena has a pretty swing from both sides of the plate and he should never stop chasing his dreams—though he probably should stop chasing pitches outside the strike zone.

YEAR	TEAM	LVL	AGE	PA	DRC+	VORP	BABIP	BRR	FRAA	WARP
2016	DUN	A+	20	431	124	17.0	.346	-1.3	SS(79): -0.1	1.5
2016	NHP	AA	20	132	74	5.3	.306	0.7	SS(29): -0.7	0.0
2017	NHP	AA	21	551	75	6.3	.294	-1.9	SS(115): -4.6, 2B(11): 0.2	-1.0
2017	TOR	MLB	21	75	60	0.4	.333	1.4	SS(20): -2.0, 2B(1): 0.1	-0.1
2018	BUF	AAA	22	268	61	-4.6	.246	-0.6	SS(43): 1.8, 2B(17): 0.9	-0.3
2018	TOR	MLB	22	108	72	0.6	.424	-1.2	SS(20): -1.3, 2B(13): -1.0	-0.3
2019	TOR	MLB	23	145	69	-1.2	.258	-0.2	3B -1, SS 0	-0.3

Richard Urena, continued

Batted Ball Distribution

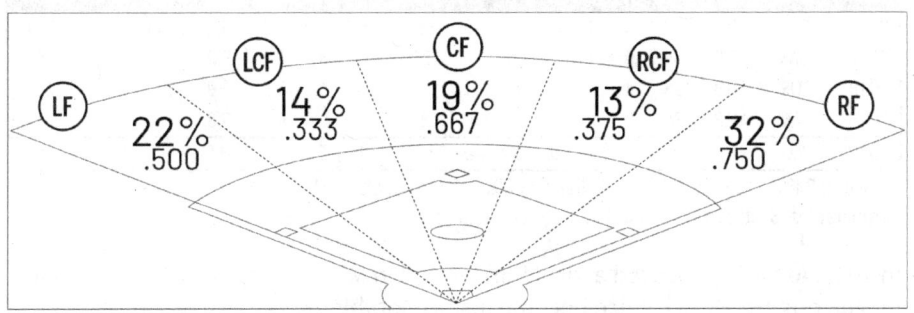

Strike Zone vs LHP   **Strike Zone vs RHP**

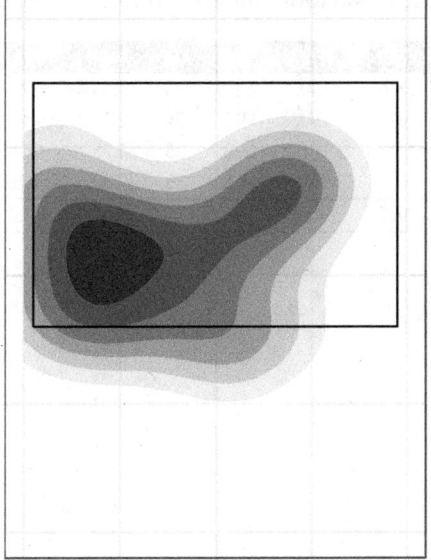

Toronto Blue Jays 2019

John Axford   RHP
Born: 04/01/83   Age: 36   Bats: R   Throws: R
Height: 6'5"   Weight: 220   Origin: Round 42, 2005 Draft (#1259 overall)

YEAR	TEAM	LVL	AGE	W	L	SV	G	GS	IP	H	HR	BB/9	K/9	K	GB%	BABIP
2016	OAK	MLB	33	6	4	3	68	0	65^2	65	6	4.1	8.2	60	56%	.311
2017	OAK	MLB	34	0	1	0	22	0	21	27	3	7.3	9.0	21	51%	.364
2018	TOR	MLB	35	4	1	0	45	1	51	44	6	3.5	8.8	50	54%	.286
2018	LAN	MLB	35	0	0	0	5	0	3^2	8	0	4.9	9.8	4	67%	.533
2019	TOR	MLB	36	2	1	0	39	0	41^2	41	5	4.2	8.5	39	51%	.308

Breakout: 24%   Improve: 46%   Collapse: 20%   Attrition: 6%   MLB: 76%
Comparables: Scott Eyre, Trever Miller, Hoyt Wilhelm

In 2011, Axford sponsored a local film festival in Milwaukee, the site of his major league origins. He has since become just as notable for his love of movies and uncanny Oscars predictions as his proclivity to shut down opposing hitters. A trade deadline move to the Dodgers was more art house horror flick than Hollywood ending, as the journeyman hurler surrendered seven earned runs in less than four innings. Oh well. At least we'll always have Milwaukee.

YEAR	TEAM	LVL	AGE	WHIP	ERA	DRA	WARP	MPH	FB%	WHF	CSP
2016	OAK	MLB	33	1.45	3.97	5.00	0.0	98.3	73.2	11.5	45.5
2017	OAK	MLB	34	2.10	6.43	7.54	-0.6	96.8	66.2	8.1	45.7
2018	TOR	MLB	35	1.25	4.41	5.13	-0.1	97.1	76.1	9.3	46.7
2018	LAN	MLB	35	2.73	17.18	6.82	-0.1	97.8	76.1	8.2	44.9
2019	TOR	MLB	36	1.46	4.43	4.54	0.2	96.1	71.7	9.6	45

John Axford, continued

Pitch Shape vs LHH	Pitch Shape vs RHH
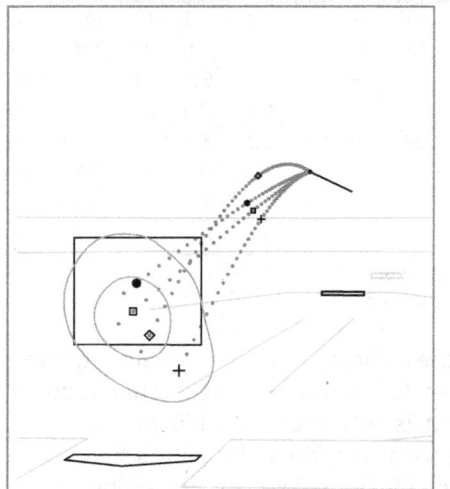	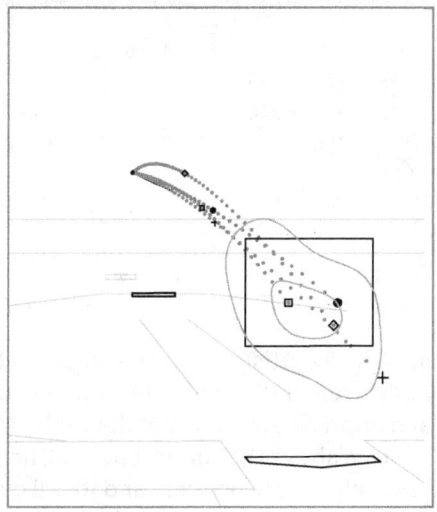

Type	Frequency	Velocity	H Movement	V Movement
● Fastball	12.4%	96.3 [112]	-3.4 [115]	-12.3 [111]
□ Sinker	61.8%	96.1 [118]	-11.6 [109]	-15.6 [116]
+ Cutter	10.9%	92.5 [122]	4.1 [113]	-22.7 [104]
▲ Changeup				
× Splitter				
▽ Slider				
◇ Curveball	14.8%	80.2 [106]	6.6 [95]	-50.6 [94]
⊕ Slow Curveball				
✻ Knuckleball				
▼ Screwball				

Danny Barnes   RHP

Born: 10/21/89   Age: 29   Bats: L   Throws: R
Height: 6'1"   Weight: 195   Origin: Round 35, 2010 Draft (#1056 overall)

YEAR	TEAM	LVL	AGE	W	L	SV	G	GS	IP	H	HR	BB/9	K/9	K	GB%	BABIP
2016	NHP	AA	26	2	1	1	24	0	35²	17	3	1.0	10.1	40	30%	.177
2016	BUF	AAA	26	1	0	5	17	0	25²	6	0	0.7	13.0	37	32%	.128
2016	TOR	MLB	26	0	0	0	12	0	13²	14	0	3.3	9.2	14	44%	.359
2017	BUF	AAA	27	0	1	2	4	0	6	6	0	0.0	12.0	8	25%	.375
2017	TOR	MLB	27	3	6	0	60	0	66	48	11	3.3	8.5	62	33%	.222
2018	BUF	AAA	28	1	1	0	7	0	8²	9	1	1.0	11.4	11	21%	.348
2018	TOR	MLB	28	3	3	0	47	0	41	47	6	4.8	8.3	38	36%	.333
2019	TOR	MLB	29	1	1	0	15	0	16	16	3	3.8	8.5	15	36%	.292

Breakout: 17%   Improve: 39%   Collapse: 17%   Attrition: 20%   MLB: 74%
Comparables: Brad Brach, Josh Fields, Arquimedes Caminero

In highwire artistry, success hinges on the ability to replicate movement. The body's center of gravity must remain low, its feet must counteract the frequent and imprecise rotations of the cable, and its arms must maintain perfect balance above the support point. One miscalculation of the cable's shift, one untimely sneeze or blink, and it's all over. Phillippe Petit was not wrong to assert, some 30-odd years after he gripped a 200-foot wire between the Twin Towers, that death itself frames the high wire.

While the middling middle reliever may never know life-or-death stakes when he steps onto the mound, he teeters along a similarly-narrow margin for error. One misstep—one ill-timed disabled list stint, one stretch of 6.00+ DRA ball—and he could lose his footing on the thin line that separates a replacement-level offering from total oblivion. Barnes found himself in just such a precarious position this spring when, after spending the winter solidifying a shaky slider, he contracted a bout of knee tendinitis that set him back for a month. His control wavered, batters started to get a handle on his once-excellent changeup, and he became no more distinguishable from a handful of warm bodies hovering between the relief corps and rotation. Luckily, the righty's path back to success appears to be as effortless as his fall from grace: simply putting one foot in front of the other, one inning at a time, with no thought to the career-ending pavement below.

YEAR	TEAM	LVL	AGE	WHIP	ERA	DRA	WARP	MPH	FB%	WHF	CSP
2016	NHP	AA	26	0.59	1.01	3.16	0.7				
2016	BUF	AAA	26	0.31	0.35	1.79	0.9				
2016	TOR	MLB	26	1.39	3.95	3.59	0.2	94.1	66.7	12.4	45.4
2017	BUF	AAA	27	1.00	3.00	1.89	0.2				
2017	TOR	MLB	27	1.09	3.55	5.51	-0.3	93.6	67.8	12.4	47.3
2018	BUF	AAA	28	1.15	5.19	3.33	0.2				
2018	TOR	MLB	28	1.68	5.71	6.18	-0.6	93.6	65.6	10.6	44.6
2019	TOR	MLB	29	1.40	5.11	5.09	0.0	93.0	66.7	11.6	45.7

Danny Barnes, continued

Pitch Shape vs LHH

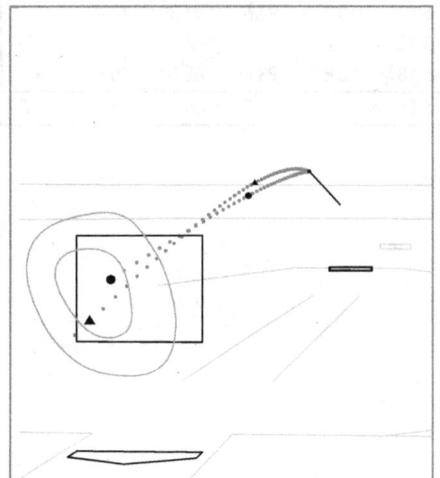

Pitch Shape vs RHH

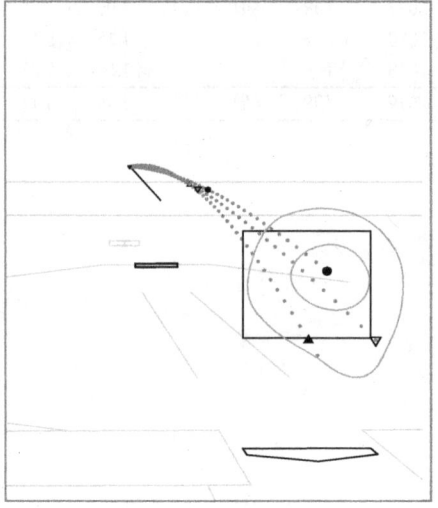

Type	Frequency	Velocity	H Movement	V Movement
● Fastball	64.9%	92.2 [99]	-10.7 [82]	-14.6 [104]
□ Sinker	0.6%	92.6 [101]	-12.4 [102]	-16.4 [113]
+ Cutter				
▲ Changeup	23.3%	80 [79]	-10.5 [104]	-36.6 [73]
✕ Splitter				
▽ Slider	11.1%	82.5 [91]	3.5 [94]	-31.5 [104]
◇ Curveball				
⊕ Slow Curveball				
✻ Knuckleball				
▼ Screwball				

Joe Biagini   RHP

Born: 05/29/90   Age: 29   Bats: R   Throws: R
Height: 6'5"   Weight: 240   Origin: Round 26, 2011 Draft (#807 overall)

YEAR	TEAM	LVL	AGE	W	L	SV	G	GS	IP	H	HR	BB/9	K/9	K	GB%	BABIP
2016	TOR	MLB	26	4	3	1	60	0	67^2	69	3	2.5	8.2	62	54%	.320
2017	BUF	AAA	27	1	1	0	4	4	17^1	13	2	3.1	7.3	14	58%	.239
2017	TOR	MLB	27	3	13	1	44	18	119^2	125	15	3.2	7.3	97	56%	.305
2018	BUF	AAA	28	0	3	0	4	4	21^2	19	1	3.3	5.4	13	45%	.257
2018	TOR	MLB	28	4	7	0	50	4	72	96	14	3.0	6.6	53	49%	.355
2019	TOR	MLB	29	3	3	0	66	0	69	70	8	3.2	7.2	56	49%	.295

Breakout: 35%   Improve: 47%   Collapse: 21%   Attrition: 20%   MLB: 83%
Comparables: Burke Badenhop, Craig Stammen, Clay Hensley

Catch Biagini on a good day, and he might tell you the story of how he unlocked his cutter after a giant talking baseball appeared to him in a drug-induced haze. Catch him on a bad day, however, and you're looking at a failed starter whose entirely sober attempts to stick in the bullpen have been underwhelming, if not downright questionable of late. The Biagini that showed up for Toronto in 2016—the one who tamed a mid-90s fastball-curve combo and whose 3.26 K/BB evidenced true starter potential—pulled off a vanishing act soon thereafter, a party trick far less entertaining than his infamous tall tales.

YEAR	TEAM	LVL	AGE	WHIP	ERA	DRA	WARP	MPH	FB%	WHF	CSP
2016	TOR	MLB	26	1.30	3.06	3.87	0.9	96.4	58.7	12.3	45.1
2017	BUF	AAA	27	1.10	3.12	4.14	0.3				
2017	TOR	MLB	27	1.40	5.34	3.98	2.0	95.5	52.9	9	47.1
2018	BUF	AAA	28	1.25	4.57	4.87	0.2				
2018	TOR	MLB	28	1.67	6.00	5.72	-0.6	96.3	60.8	9.5	45.6
2019	TOR	MLB	29	1.36	4.40	4.54	0.5	95.3	56.9	9.8	46

Joe Biagini, continued

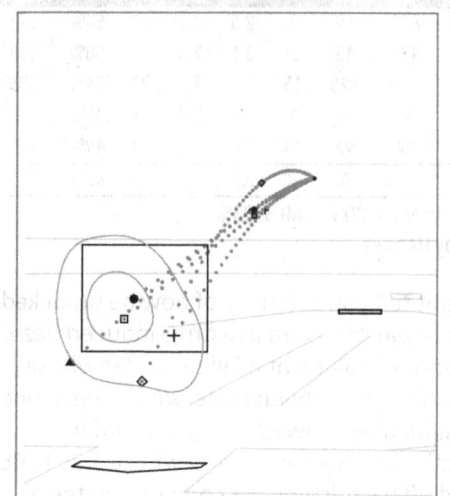
Pitch Shape vs LHH

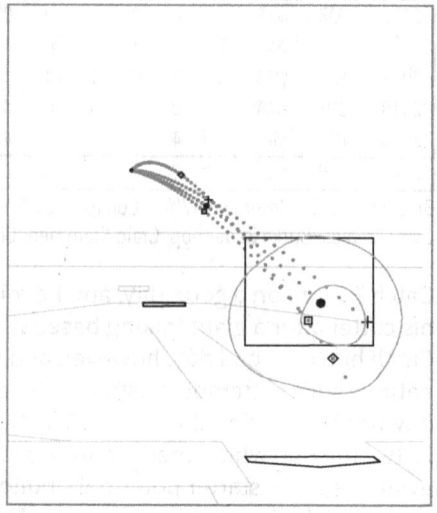
Pitch Shape vs RHH

Type	Frequency	Velocity	H Movement	V Movement
● Fastball	17.1%	94.4 [106]	-7 [99]	-13.3 [108]
☐ Sinker	43.7%	94.8 [112]	-10 [121]	-13.9 [121]
+ Cutter	15.5%	89.8 [106]	2.4 [103]	-23.5 [101]
▲ Changeup	9.8%	86.9 [106]	-12.4 [94]	-25.6 [105]
✕ Splitter				
▽ Slider				
◇ Curveball	13.9%	78.5 [100]	7.6 [99]	-56.6 [81]
✜ Slow Curveball				
✱ Knuckleball				
▼ Screwball				

Ryan Borucki LHP

Born: 03/31/94 Age: 25 Bats: L Throws: L
Height: 6'4" Weight: 175 Origin: Round 15, 2012 Draft (#475 overall)

YEAR	TEAM	LVL	AGE	W	L	SV	G	GS	IP	H	HR	BB/9	K/9	K	GB%	BABIP
2016	DUN	A+	22	1	4	0	6	6	20	40	10	5.4	4.5	10	48%	.395
2016	LNS	A	22	10	4	0	20	20	115^2	105	1	2.0	8.3	107	51%	.322
2017	DUN	A+	23	6	5	0	19	18	98	95	5	2.5	10.0	109	52%	.342
2017	NHP	AA	23	2	3	0	7	7	46^1	31	2	1.6	8.2	42	58%	.236
2017	BUF	AAA	23	0	0	0	1	1	6	6	0	1.5	9.0	6	50%	.375
2018	BUF	AAA	24	6	5	0	13	13	77	62	6	3.3	6.8	58	52%	.255
2018	TOR	MLB	24	4	6	0	17	17	97^2	96	7	3.0	6.2	67	49%	.291
2019	TOR	MLB	25	7	9	0	23	23	131	137	20	3.3	6.9	101	47%	.294

Breakout: 14%   Improve: 40%   Collapse: 22%   Attrition: 30%   MLB: 80%
Comparables: Adalberto Mejia, Chris Archer, Robbie Ross

We can repeat "good when healthy" ad nauseam, but the caution surrounding Borucki's call-up is valid, and not just because the fresh-faced southpaw underwent Tommy John surgery at the ripe old age of 19 in 2013. Even when firing on all cylinders, Borucki lacks the kind of standout tools that will help separate him from the rest of the pack—in other words, he's hardly what you'd describe as the second coming of lefty hurlers Clayton Kershaw or Madison Bumgarner. Though what he lacks in overwhelming talent, he makes up for with consistency (peep the 11 quality starts that formed the bulk of his performance in 2018) and a no-nonsense, low-90s fastball. While the jury's still out on his major-league ceiling, he should be able to keep the rookie jitters at bay long enough to earn another long look in 2019.

YEAR	TEAM	LVL	AGE	WHIP	ERA	DRA	WARP	MPH	FB%	WHF	CSP
2016	DUN	A+	22	2.60	14.40	7.78	-0.5				
2016	LNS	A	22	1.13	2.41	3.36	2.3				
2017	DUN	A+	23	1.24	3.58	3.09	2.5				
2017	NHP	AA	23	0.84	1.94	3.45	0.9				
2017	BUF	AAA	23	1.17	0.00	3.02	0.2				
2018	BUF	AAA	24	1.17	3.27	3.99	1.4				
2018	TOR	MLB	24	1.32	3.87	4.53	0.9	93.1	58.7	8.7	49.1
2019	TOR	MLB	25	1.41	4.86	5.14	0.4	92.8	60.1	8.9	50.3

Toronto Blue Jays 2019

Ryan Borucki, continued

Pitch Shape vs LHH

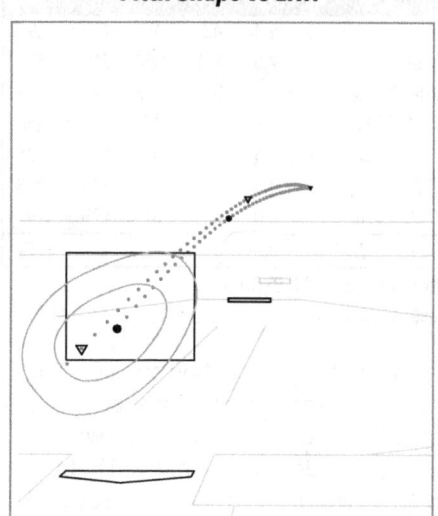

Pitch Shape vs RHH

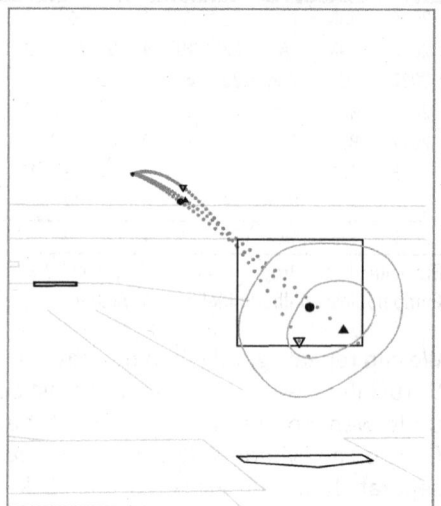

Type	Frequency	Velocity	H Movement	V Movement
● Fastball	58.7%	91.9 [98]	15.6 [59]	-20.8 [84]
☐ Sinker				
+ Cutter				
▲ Changeup	23.3%	83.7 [94]	13.1 [90]	-24.2 [109]
✕ Splitter				
▽ Slider	18.0%	80.2 [81]	-3.5 [94]	-40.2 [79]
◇ Curveball				
⊕ Slow Curveball				
✳ Knuckleball				
▼ Screwball				

Clay Buchholz RHP

Born: 08/14/84 Age: 34 Bats: L Throws: R
Height: 6'3" Weight: 190 Origin: Round 1, 2005 Draft (#42 overall)

YEAR	TEAM	LVL	AGE	W	L	SV	G	GS	IP	H	HR	BB/9	K/9	K	GB%	BABIP
2016	BOS	MLB	31	8	10	0	37	21	139^1	130	21	3.6	6.0	93	42%	.263
2017	PHI	MLB	32	0	1	0	2	2	7^1	16	1	3.7	6.1	5	31%	.484
2018	OMA	AAA	33	1	0	0	2	2	11^1	9	2	4.0	3.2	4	55%	.194
2018	RNO	AAA	33	0	1	0	2	2	11^2	12	0	3.9	7.7	10	40%	.324
2018	ARI	MLB	33	7	2	0	16	16	98^1	80	9	2.0	7.4	81	43%	.256
2019	TOR	MLB	34	4	5	0	13	13	74	77	12	3.4	6.7	55	41%	.291

Breakout: 11% Improve: 35% Collapse: 23% Attrition: 14% MLB: 89%
Comparables: Whitey Ford, Doug Fister, Tim Hudson

Late last winter, Buchholz was enjoying a sojourn in Denmark when he was awoken to the sound of broken glass. He jolted from bed, grabbed an axe-handled bat with no idea of how to swing it and ventured downstairs in the dark. Seeing no intruders, he opened the front door to find a collection of broken dinner plates littered about. His elbow tinged and Buchholz wondered what kind of sick joke had just been played at his expense. He shut the door and turned to his favorite web browser, Altavista, searching for answers. He quickly found that the Danish throw broken dinner plates at houses on New Year's Eve as a wishing of good luck. Feeling renewed and, frankly, relieved, Buchholz went back to bed. "This year is going to be different," he said. Buchholz proceeded to pitch incredibly well for the Diamondbacks before finishing the season on the disabled list. It really was a different year, and also, it wasn't.

YEAR	TEAM	LVL	AGE	WHIP	ERA	DRA	WARP	MPH	FB%	WHF	CSP
2016	BOS	MLB	31	1.33	4.78	5.29	0.0	94.4	63.4	10	45.7
2017	PHI	MLB	32	2.59	12.27	6.77	-0.1	92.1	65.2	6.5	49.7
2018	OMA	AAA	33	1.24	1.59	8.98	-0.4				
2018	RNO	AAA	33	1.46	5.40	4.67	0.1				
2018	ARI	MLB	33	1.04	2.01	3.74	1.8	91.7	65.9	10.5	50.4
2019	TOR	MLB	34	1.40	4.93	5.20	0.2	91.8	63.7	10	48.3

Clay Buchholz, continued

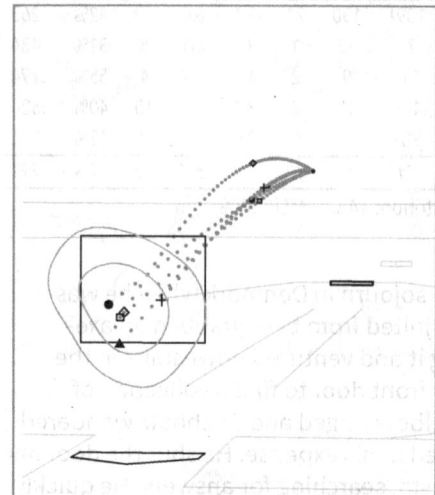
Pitch Shape vs LHH

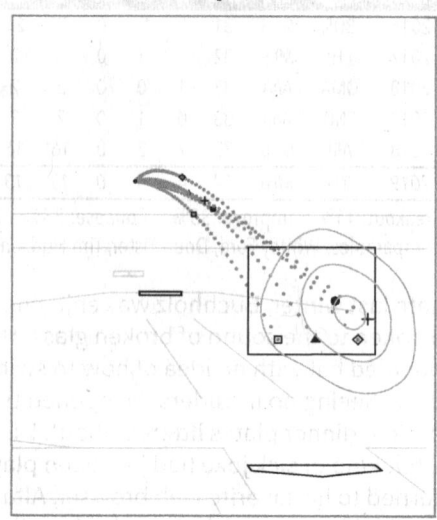
Pitch Shape vs RHH

Type	Frequency	Velocity	H Movement	V Movement
● Fastball	24.5%	90.7 [94]	-8.1 [94]	-16.3 [98]
□ Sinker	16.8%	90.4 [90]	-12.2 [103]	-20.7 [99]
+ Cutter	24.6%	86.2 [85]	2.6 [104]	-25.1 [94]
▲ Changeup	16.9%	77.8 [70]	-7.6 [120]	-34.6 [78]
✕ Splitter				
▽ Slider				
◇ Curveball	17.2%	76.2 [92]	12.3 [119]	-52.8 [89]
✦ Slow Curveball				
✱ Knuckleball				
▼ Screwball				

Samuel Gaviglio   RHP

Born: 05/22/90   Age: 29   Bats: R   Throws: R
Height: 6'2"   Weight: 195   Origin: Round 5, 2011 Draft (#170 overall)

YEAR	TEAM	LVL	AGE	W	L	SV	G	GS	IP	H	HR	BB/9	K/9	K	GB%	BABIP
2016	WTN	AA	26	5	5	0	18	17	102	104	7	1.9	6.4	73	54%	.303
2016	TAC	AAA	26	3	2	0	10	9	63	59	7	2.0	7.1	50	50%	.278
2017	SEA	MLB	27	3	5	0	12	11	62^1	63	15	3.0	5.8	40	49%	.265
2017	TAC	AAA	27	3	6	0	13	13	72	72	5	1.5	7.1	57	54%	.302
2017	KCA	MLB	27	1	0	0	4	2	12	13	1	3.8	6.8	9	56%	.316
2018	BUF	AAA	28	0	0	0	5	5	29	21	4	1.2	9.0	29	46%	.243
2018	TOR	MLB	28	3	10	0	26	24	123^2	140	21	2.8	7.6	105	50%	.313
2019	TOR	MLB	29	5	5	0	54	8	90^2	90	12	2.8	7.3	74	48%	.292

Breakout: 22%   Improve: 29%   Collapse: 24%   Attrition: 19%   MLB: 62%
Comparables: Philip Humber, Chris Rusin, Mike Bolsinger

Nothing Gaviglio does should work in the majors. He shouldn't be able to hold down a rotation spot with a fastball that barely grazes 88 mph. He shouldn't be able to dance around the strike zone 59.2 percent of the time. He shouldn't be able to get hitters to chase bad pitches with any kind of regularity, and he shouldn't treat that ability as a viable in-game strategy. One look at the righty's wild animal of a slider is enough to put most of those fears to rest, however. He hasn't fully tamed the pitch yet, but a dash of lateral movement caused 54 percent of batters to chase after it in 2018 and his vastly-improved whiff rate is a harbinger of better things to come. There's no guarantee that the Blue Jays will keep a rotation spot free for the starter moving forward, but he possesses the tools and creative potential to carve his own unorthodox path to success.

YEAR	TEAM	LVL	AGE	WHIP	ERA	DRA	WARP	MPH	FB%	WHF	CSP
2016	WTN	AA	26	1.24	4.15	3.16	2.3				
2016	TAC	AAA	26	1.16	3.71	3.73	1.1				
2017	SEA	MLB	27	1.35	4.62	5.69	-0.1	90.3	56.6	7.3	50.3
2017	TAC	AAA	27	1.17	3.88	3.53	1.7				
2017	KCA	MLB	27	1.50	3.00	5.12	0.1	91.0	59.5	10	51.2
2018	BUF	AAA	28	0.86	1.86	3.81	0.6				
2018	TOR	MLB	28	1.44	5.31	4.90	0.6	90.2	56	9.2	46.7
2019	TOR	MLB	29	1.31	4.32	4.49	0.8	89.6	56.3	8.8	48.4

Toronto Blue Jays 2019

Samuel Gaviglio, continued

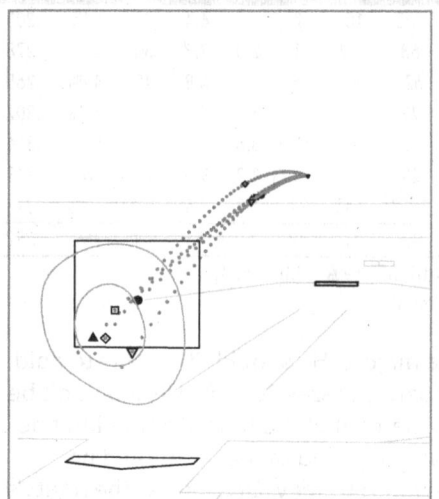
Pitch Shape vs LHH

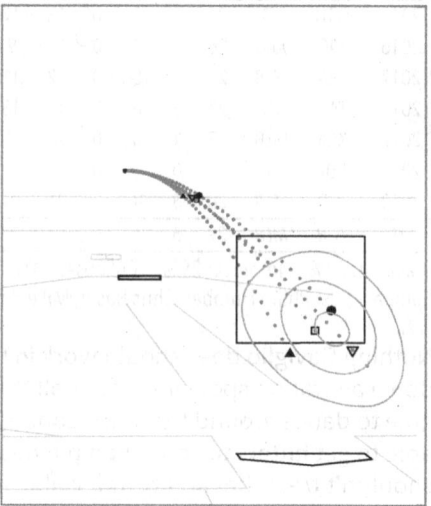
Pitch Shape vs RHH

Type	Frequency	Velocity	H Movement	V Movement
● Fastball	8.3%	88.5 [87]	-9.2 [88]	-21.8 [81]
☐ Sinker	47.7%	88.5 [80]	-12.2 [104]	-24.2 [87]
+ Cutter				
▲ Changeup	9.8%	83.2 [91]	-11.7 [98]	-30.9 [89]
✕ Splitter				
▽ Slider	28.6%	83.5 [96]	2.4 [89]	-32.3 [102]
◇ Curveball	5.6%	78.4 [100]	6.6 [95]	-43.5 [110]
⊕ Slow Curveball				
✱ Knuckleball				
▼ Screwball				

Ken Giles   RHP

Born: 09/20/90   Age: 28   Bats: R   Throws: R
Height: 6'2"   Weight: 205   Origin: Round 7, 2011 Draft (#241 overall)

YEAR	TEAM	LVL	AGE	W	L	SV	G	GS	IP	H	HR	BB/9	K/9	K	GB%	BABIP
2016	HOU	MLB	25	2	5	15	69	0	65^2	60	8	3.4	14.0	102	41%	.349
2017	HOU	MLB	26	1	3	34	63	0	62^2	44	4	3.0	11.9	83	45%	.290
2018	HOU	MLB	27	0	2	12	34	0	30^2	36	2	0.9	9.1	31	37%	.366
2018	TOR	MLB	27	0	1	14	21	0	19^2	18	4	1.8	10.1	22	54%	.269
2019	*TOR*	*MLB*	*28*	*3*	*3*	*30*	*56*	*0*	*59*	*55*	*8*	*3.1*	*9.8*	*65*	*42%*	*.302*

Breakout: 28%   Improve: 43%   Collapse: 31%   Attrition: 11%   MLB: 90%
Comparables: Cody Allen, Francisco Rodriguez, Jordan Walden

"I'm actually enjoying the game more than I did for my entire tenure in Houston," Giles told reporters following his midseason shift from the defending champion Astros to the defending fourth-place Blue Jays. "It's kind of weird to say that because I won a World Series with that team." A.J. Hinch vehemently denied the charges, but there was no question that his former closer felt a degree of comfort in Toronto that he hadn't been able to grab hold of in Houston. Like a college kid enjoying the luxuries of homemade cooking and parent-folded laundry on winter break, Giles perhaps relaxed into his new role a little too easily. His peripherals were as strong as ever, but his ERA ballooned back up above four, and his WARP dipped below one for the first time in his career. The scorching heater that headlines his pitch repertoire also lost a little gas in the chilly Canadian clime. It might be said here that comfort and complacency are close neighbors—an adage better taken to heart early than late.

YEAR	TEAM	LVL	AGE	WHIP	ERA	DRA	WARP	MPH	FB%	WHF	CSP
2016	HOU	MLB	25	1.29	4.11	2.10	2.2	100.0	52.1	20.9	42.4
2017	HOU	MLB	26	1.04	2.30	2.85	1.6	99.7	52.8	17.2	49.1
2018	HOU	MLB	27	1.27	4.99	3.42	0.5	98.9	57.7	16.9	51.8
2018	TOR	MLB	27	1.12	4.12	3.18	0.4	98.9	61.3	16.3	48.9
2019	*TOR*	*MLB*	*28*	*1.30*	*3.67*	*3.95*	*0.8*	*98.9*	*55.1*	*18.2*	*48.4*

Toronto Blue Jays 2019

Ken Giles, continued

Pitch Shape vs LHH   **Pitch Shape vs RHH**

Type	Frequency	Velocity	H Movement	V Movement
● Fastball	59.1%	97.6 [116]	-7.9 [94]	-11.1 [115]
☐ Sinker				
+ Cutter				
▲ Changeup				
✕ Splitter				
▽ Slider	40.9%	86.9 [111]	0.1 [79]	-30.6 [107]
◇ Curveball				
⊕ Slow Curveball				
✻ Knuckleball				
▼ Screwball				

Mark Leiter RHP

Born: 03/13/91 Age: 28 Bats: R Throws: R
Height: 6'0" Weight: 195 Origin: Round 22, 2013 Draft (#661 overall)

YEAR	TEAM	LVL	AGE	W	L	SV	G	GS	IP	H	HR	BB/9	K/9	K	GB%	BABIP
2016	REA	AA	25	6	3	1	23	17	103^2	91	9	2.6	8.2	94	46%	.288
2017	LEH	AAA	26	2	1	0	7	5	30	27	5	1.8	11.4	38	53%	.297
2017	PHI	MLB	26	3	6	0	27	11	90^2	90	18	3.1	8.3	84	50%	.282
2018	PHI	MLB	27	0	1	0	12	0	16^2	22	5	4.3	7.0	13	52%	.298
2018	LEH	AAA	27	3	1	0	20	0	28^1	28	3	4.1	9.5	30	45%	.316
2018	TOR	MLB	27	0	0	0	8	0	6^2	13	2	5.4	12.1	9	36%	.478
2019	TOR	MLB	28	3	3	0	24	8	59^1	60	8	3.7	8.7	58	44%	.306

Breakout: 25% Improve: 46% Collapse: 13% Attrition: 27% MLB: 69%
Comparables: Dan Meyer, Sam LeCure, Tyler Lyons

Elevated by dint of his family connections—father and former major-league pitcher, Mark Sr., and uncle and Blue Jays southpaw, Al—Leiter may have felt the legacy talents breathing down his neck when he was claimed off of waivers and given a fresh start in Toronto last September. Evidently, the Blue Jays didn't share the same high hopes for the righty and the substandard fastball in his tool belt. Leiter's value as a multifaceted swingman was compromised when he converted to full-time relief in 2018. His heater went up a few ticks on the radar gun, but what little speed he gained was negated by his inability to control balls and strikes. Another stint in Triple-A should help him pare down an overloaded pitch repertoire and sharpen his command, but it's anyone's guess as to when he'll be able to slice into a major-league strike zone again.

YEAR	TEAM	LVL	AGE	WHIP	ERA	DRA	WARP	MPH	FB%	WHF	CSP
2016	REA	AA	25	1.17	3.39	3.15	2.3				
2017	LEH	AAA	26	1.10	4.20	2.62	1.0				
2017	PHI	MLB	26	1.33	4.96	5.43	0.0	92.5	55.6	9.4	47.3
2018	PHI	MLB	27	1.80	5.40	7.45	-0.5	92.8	48.7	11.4	46.9
2018	LEH	AAA	27	1.45	3.81	4.76	0.1				
2018	TOR	MLB	27	2.55	13.50	9.13	-0.3	92.2	48.7	9.3	42
2019	TOR	MLB	28	1.42	4.65	4.77	0.4	92.0	54	9.8	46.5

Mark Leiter, continued

Pitch Shape vs LHH

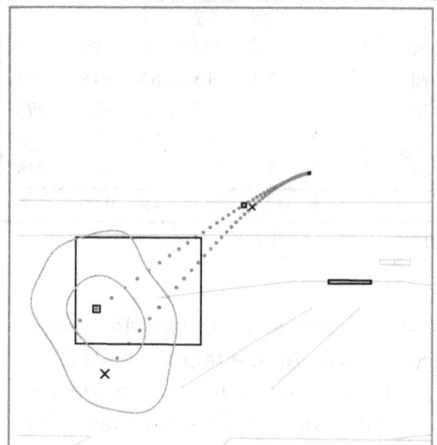

Pitch Shape vs RHH

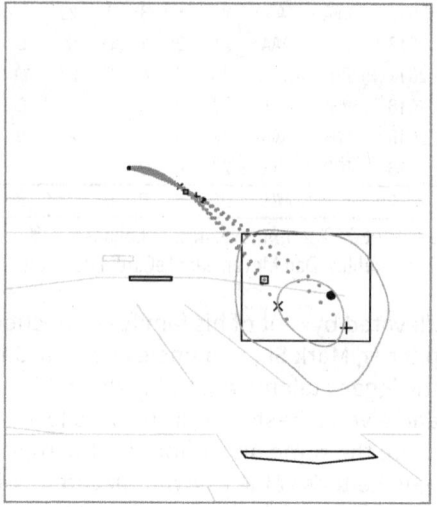

Type	Frequency	Velocity	H Movement	V Movement
● Fastball	25.9%	91.8 [98]	-4.6 [110]	-13.5 [107]
□ Sinker	25.9%	91.6 [96]	-11.5 [109]	-17.3 [110]
+ Cutter	13.3%	87.4 [92]	2.8 [105]	-26 [91]
▲ Changeup				
✕ Splitter	25.1%	84.9 [96]	-5.3 [111]	-28.4 [105]
▽ Slider				
◇ Curveball	9.9%	73.4 [81]	7.3 [98]	-61.3 [70]
⊕ Slow Curveball				
✳ Knuckleball				
▼ Screwball				

Tim Mayza LHP

Born: 01/15/92   Age: 27   Bats: L   Throws: L
Height: 6'3"   Weight: 220   Origin: Round 12, 2013 Draft (#355 overall)

YEAR	TEAM	LVL	AGE	W	L	SV	G	GS	IP	H	HR	BB/9	K/9	K	GB%	BABIP
2016	NHP	AA	24	1	3	0	14	0	15^1	16	0	8.8	7.6	13	61%	.348
2016	DUN	A+	24	2	0	4	28	0	48^2	36	1	2.8	9.6	52	56%	.267
2017	NHP	AA	25	1	1	4	29	0	33^1	32	5	4.1	11.3	42	42%	.325
2017	BUF	AAA	25	1	1	0	11	0	19^1	16	0	3.3	7.4	16	33%	.276
2017	TOR	MLB	25	1	0	0	19	0	17	24	3	2.1	14.3	27	42%	.467
2018	BUF	AAA	26	6	2	1	20	0	25^2	26	2	3.9	12.6	36	42%	.400
2018	TOR	MLB	26	2	0	0	37	0	35^2	33	3	3.5	10.1	40	46%	.326
2019	TOR	MLB	27	2	2	0	41	0	42	40	6	4.5	9.8	47	45%	.305

Breakout: 15%   Improve: 21%   Collapse: 21%   Attrition: 33%   MLB: 53%
Comparables: Juan Minaya, Chris Hatcher, Luis Perdomo

Mayza found his niche the way Ross Geller found his "sound": with abundant enthusiasm and mixed results. While his signature 90-mph slider was as intriguing as it was effective, the lefty needed more than a go-to out pitch (the backbeat to Ross' wordless sound poems, as it were) in order to earn a permanent post in the bullpen. After another year pinballing between Triple-A and the majors, he finally started to mature beyond an exclusive LOOGY role, but the rest of his future remains clouded by prolonged struggles with an erratic four-seamer—something, it could be argued, as essential as melody to music.

YEAR	TEAM	LVL	AGE	WHIP	ERA	DRA	WARP	MPH	FB%	WHF	CSP
2016	NHP	AA	24	2.02	4.11	4.52	0.0				
2016	DUN	A+	24	1.05	1.66	4.22	0.5				
2017	NHP	AA	25	1.41	4.59	3.21	0.6				
2017	BUF	AAA	25	1.19	0.93	4.26	0.2				
2017	TOR	MLB	25	1.65	6.88	2.61	0.5	95.8	49.4	17.1	40.1
2018	BUF	AAA	26	1.44	4.56	3.18	0.6				
2018	TOR	MLB	26	1.32	3.28	3.76	0.5	95.7	56	15.1	43.6
2019	TOR	MLB	27	1.46	4.42	4.56	0.3	95.2	54.6	15.9	42.6

Toronto Blue Jays 2019

Tim Mayza, continued

Pitch Shape vs LHH   **Pitch Shape vs RHH**

Type	Frequency	Velocity	H Movement	V Movement
● Fastball	56.0%	94.3 [106]	8.5 [91]	-13.8 [106]
☐ Sinker				
+ Cutter				
▲ Changeup				
✕ Splitter				
▽ Slider	44.0%	86.6 [109]	-1.3 [84]	-30.6 [107]
◇ Curveball				
⊕ Slow Curveball				
✳ Knuckleball				
▼ Screwball				

Bud Norris RHP

Born: 03/02/85   Age: 34   Bats: R   Throws: R
Height: 6'0"   Weight: 215   Origin: Round 6, 2006 Draft (#189 overall)

YEAR	TEAM	LVL	AGE	W	L	SV	G	GS	IP	H	HR	BB/9	K/9	K	GB%	BABIP
2016	ATL	MLB	31	3	7	0	22	10	70¹	68	6	3.6	7.7	60	53%	.302
2016	LAN	MLB	31	3	3	0	13	9	42²	48	8	4.4	8.9	42	45%	.328
2017	ANA	MLB	32	2	6	19	60	3	62	56	8	3.9	10.7	74	45%	.310
2018	SLN	MLB	33	3	6	28	64	0	57²	51	8	3.3	10.5	67	45%	.299
2019	TOR	MLB	34	2	2	0	41	0	42	38	5	3.8	9.7	46	45%	.294

Breakout: 26%   Improve: 48%   Collapse: 17%   Attrition: 7%   MLB: 86%
Comparables: Jesse Chavez, Jakie May, Steve Carlton

When Norris finally gave up on remaining a big-league starter, his career drew new and fresh breath. He repositioned a cutter that had risen and fallen among the ranks of his secondary offerings as his primary pitch. After finding success that way in 2017, he cut his slider almost out of the mix in 2018, feeling that returning to an old sinker would give him a pitch that wiggled in either direction, relative to his four-seamer. He faded badly down the stretch, but Norris's bulldog approach and those three pitches playing off one another spell sustainable success as a short-burst reliever. By all accounts, Norris's red-ass clubhouse presence is polarizing, but on the mound, he's much better suited to his present role than to his preferred one.

YEAR	TEAM	LVL	AGE	WHIP	ERA	DRA	WARP	MPH	FB%	WHF	CSP
2016	ATL	MLB	31	1.36	4.22	4.97	0.3	96.0	50.6	10.3	45.6
2016	LAN	MLB	31	1.62	6.54	4.19	0.5	95.8	50.6	11.4	47.4
2017	ANA	MLB	32	1.34	4.21	3.90	0.9	95.5	44.5	13.8	43.5
2018	SLN	MLB	33	1.25	3.59	3.69	0.8	96.0	56.1	13.4	46.4
2019	TOR	MLB	34	1.30	3.75	4.02	0.6	94.7	49.9	12.3	44.7

Bud Norris, continued

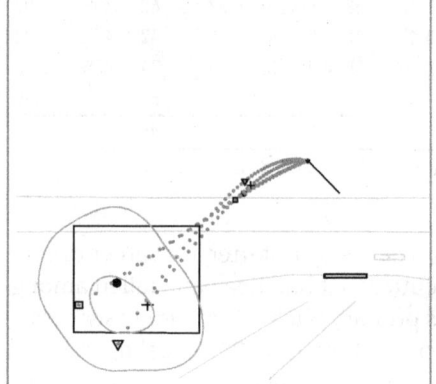
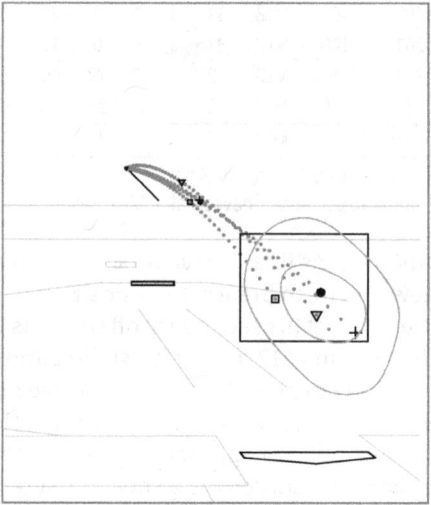

Type	Frequency	Velocity	H Movement	V Movement
● Fastball	29.4%	94.9 [108]	-5.2 [107]	-11.9 [112]
☐ Sinker	26.7%	95.3 [114]	-11.1 [112]	-13.7 [122]
+ Cutter	36.0%	90.2 [109]	3.7 [111]	-24.9 [95]
▲ Changeup	0.2%	88.9 [114]	-11.3 [100]	-21.5 [117]
✕ Splitter				
▽ Slider	7.7%	84.6 [101]	5.5 [103]	-37.8 [86]
◇ Curveball				
⊕ Slow Curveball				
✱ Knuckleball				
▼ Screwball				

Thomas Pannone LHP

Born: 04/28/94   Age: 25   Bats: L   Throws: L
Height: 6'0"   Weight: 195   Origin: Round 9, 2013 Draft (#261 overall)

YEAR	TEAM	LVL	AGE	W	L	SV	G	GS	IP	H	HR	BB/9	K/9	K	GB%	BABIP
2016	LKC	A	22	5	5	0	17	17	89^1	73	7	2.5	8.5	84	39%	.269
2016	LYN	A+	22	3	0	0	8	7	43^2	31	1	3.3	7.8	38	40%	.254
2017	LYN	A+	23	2	0	0	5	5	27^2	10	0	2.3	12.7	39	48%	.212
2017	AKR	AA	23	6	1	0	14	14	82^1	67	5	2.3	8.9	81	37%	.281
2017	NHP	AA	23	1	2	0	6	6	34^2	31	9	2.1	7.5	29	38%	.232
2018	NHP	AA	24	0	0	0	2	2	9	9	1	5.0	12.0	12	29%	.348
2018	BUF	AAA	24	0	3	0	6	6	36^2	40	8	1.7	9.8	40	24%	.327
2018	TOR	MLB	24	4	1	0	12	6	43	37	7	3.1	6.1	29	36%	.234
2019	TOR	MLB	25	4	5	0	13	13	74	76	15	3.3	7.7	63	35%	.289

Breakout: 15%   Improve: 30%   Collapse: 19%   Attrition: 34%   MLB: 60%
Comparables: Michael Bowden, Scott Lewis, Eric Skoglund

The Blue Jays put the kibosh on Pannone's petition for a rotation spot when he was slapped with an 80-game suspension for the misuse of anabolic steroids. Following several months of mandated rehab, the left-handed swingman returned to the team in mid-August and began to show legitimate flashes of starter potential after turning in four quality performances over six assigned starts. While the command and control on his fastball masks a noted lack of oomph, he complements the pitch with a handful of passable, if not decent secondaries, and sequences well enough to get around most big-league batters.

YEAR	TEAM	LVL	AGE	WHIP	ERA	DRA	WARP	MPH	FB%	WHF	CSP
2016	LKC	A	22	1.10	3.02	3.33	1.8				
2016	LYN	A+	22	1.08	1.65	3.81	0.8				
2017	LYN	A+	23	0.61	0.00	2.91	0.8				
2017	AKR	AA	23	1.07	2.62	3.73	1.4				
2017	NHP	AA	23	1.12	3.63	4.15	0.4				
2018	NHP	AA	24	1.56	3.00	3.84	0.2				
2018	BUF	AAA	24	1.28	4.91	5.29	0.1				
2018	TOR	MLB	24	1.21	4.19	5.89	-0.3	90.1	64.2	10.4	50.6
2019	TOR	MLB	25	1.38	5.23	5.54	-0.1	89.8	65.7	10.6	51.8

Toronto Blue Jays 2019

Thomas Pannone, continued

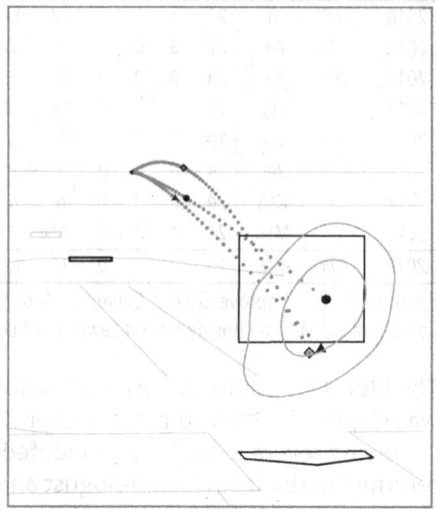

Type	Frequency	Velocity	H Movement	V Movement
● Fastball	64.2%	88.4 [87]	8.8 [90]	-16.2 [99]
☐ Sinker				
+ Cutter				
▲ Changeup	17.6%	82.3 [88]	14 [85]	-29.6 [93]
✕ Splitter				
▽ Slider				
◇ Curveball	18.3%	70.6 [71]	-12.5 [120]	-57.3 [79]
⊕ Slow Curveball				
✻ Knuckleball				
▼ Screwball				

Sean Reid-Foley RHP

Born: 08/30/95 Age: 23 Bats: R Throws: R
Height: 6'3" Weight: 220 Origin: Round 2, 2014 Draft (#49 overall)

YEAR	TEAM	LVL	AGE	W	L	SV	G	GS	IP	H	HR	BB/9	K/9	K	GB%	BABIP
2016	LNS	A	20	4	3	0	11	11	58	43	2	3.4	9.2	59	52%	.277
2016	DUN	A+	20	6	2	0	10	10	57^1	35	2	2.5	11.1	71	49%	.254
2017	NHP	AA	21	10	11	0	27	27	132^2	145	22	3.6	8.3	122	42%	.318
2018	NHP	AA	22	5	0	0	8	8	44^1	27	3	4.1	10.6	52	55%	.240
2018	BUF	AAA	22	7	5	0	16	16	85^1	76	5	3.2	10.3	98	43%	.318
2018	TOR	MLB	22	2	4	0	7	7	33^1	31	6	5.7	11.3	42	36%	.312
2019	TOR	MLB	23	4	4	0	11	11	62^2	58	8	3.8	9.3	65	43%	.294

Breakout: 22%   Improve: 33%   Collapse: 16%   Attrition: 34%   MLB: 64%
Comparables: Michael Fulmer, Zach Davies, Lucas Giolito

There are few things more unsettling than undeniable talent marred by inconsistent results. The hard-throwing righty landed on the club's top-ten prospect list five years in a row with an above-average slider, a fastball that gets a healthy swing-and-miss rate (when, and only when, it finds the strike zone) and a handful of tertiary pitches with the potential to slant average. With still-spotty control and limited opportunities in the majors, however—opportunities that have no doubt been compromised in part by his uninspired track record in the upper minors—it may be a stretch to expect him to reach his ceiling as a mid-rotation piece anytime soon.

YEAR	TEAM	LVL	AGE	WHIP	ERA	DRA	WARP	MPH	FB%	WHF	CSP
2016	LNS	A	20	1.12	2.95	3.51	1.1				
2016	DUN	A+	20	0.89	2.67	2.90	1.7				
2017	NHP	AA	21	1.49	5.09	5.63	-0.7				
2018	NHP	AA	22	1.06	2.03	3.65	0.9				
2018	BUF	AAA	22	1.24	3.90	3.19	2.3				
2018	TOR	MLB	22	1.56	5.13	4.95	0.1	95.7	63.2	13.1	47.3
2019	TOR	MLB	23	1.34	4.23	4.46	0.7	95.6	65.5	13.5	49

Toronto Blue Jays 2019

Sean Reid-Foley, continued

Pitch Shape vs LHH

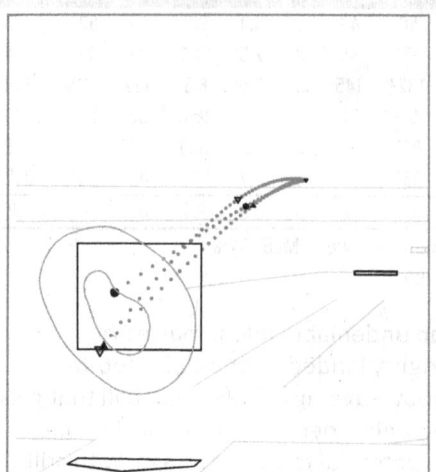

Pitch Shape vs RHH

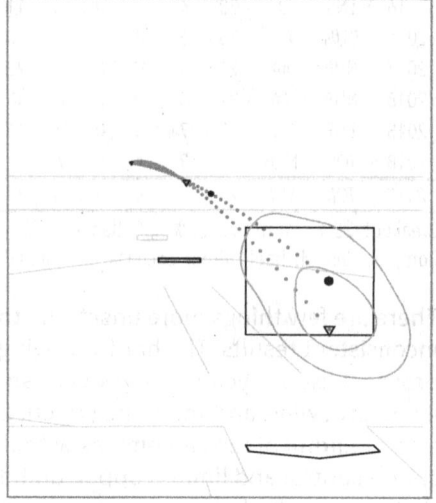

Type	Frequency	Velocity	H Movement	V Movement
● Fastball	63.2%	94.2 [105]	-10.3 [83]	-14.8 [103]
☐ Sinker				
+ Cutter				
▲ Changeup	7.9%	85.7 [101]	-13 [91]	-30.3 [91]
✕ Splitter				
▽ Slider	23.6%	84 [98]	5.2 [102]	-35.2 [93]
◇ Curveball	5.3%	81.9 [113]	11.3 [114]	-42.7 [112]
⊕ Slow Curveball				
✳ Knuckleball				
▼ Screwball				

Clayton Richard LHP

Born: 09/12/83 Age: 35 Bats: L Throws: L
Height: 6'5" Weight: 240 Origin: Round 8, 2005 Draft (#245 overall)

YEAR	TEAM	LVL	AGE	W	L	SV	G	GS	IP	H	HR	BB/9	K/9	K	GB%	BABIP
2016	CHN	MLB	32	0	1	1	25	0	14	23	0	4.5	4.5	7	73%	.411
2016	SDN	MLB	32	3	3	0	11	9	53²	58	4	4.0	5.7	34	64%	.314
2017	SDN	MLB	33	8	15	0	32	32	197¹	240	24	2.7	6.9	151	60%	.351
2018	SDN	MLB	34	7	11	0	27	27	158²	159	19	3.4	6.1	108	58%	.289
2019	TOR	MLB	35	5	7	0	18	18	95	103	12	3.6	6.4	68	57%	.304

Breakout: 10% Improve: 26% Collapse: 17% Attrition: 11% MLB: 67%
Comparables: Jerome Williams, Roberto Hernandez, Kevin Correia

Richard led the National League in losses and hits allowed in 2017, which was apparently enough to earn the Opening Day nod last year. He's the sort of breed who might fool fans were they never allowed to see his numbers. A craftsman on the mound, both his distinct, sweeping curveball and elite pickoff move lend cover to a pitcher who peaked as a backend starter years ago and tumbled considerably from there.

Those pesky statistics tell the story, though. Richard has accrued a total of 2.4 WARP in more than 1200 career innings, and given that he led the league in runs allowed last year, it doesn't appear he's improving with age. San Diego has a half dozen rookies pining for starts and several more interesting arms who deserve a longer look, which means that Richard's time in town should conclude soon. Never great and rarely notable, he sure was *there* an awful lot.

YEAR	TEAM	LVL	AGE	WHIP	ERA	DRA	WARP	MPH	FB%	WHF	CSP
2016	CHN	MLB	32	2.14	6.43	5.72	-0.1	94.2	82.3	6.5	45.4
2016	SDN	MLB	32	1.53	2.52	5.60	-0.2	93.1	82.3	9.8	44.2
2017	SDN	MLB	33	1.52	4.79	5.18	0.9	92.4	69.3	9.6	45.8
2018	SDN	MLB	34	1.38	5.33	4.91	0.7	91.7	66	8.9	48.8
2019	TOR	MLB	35	1.51	4.63	4.89	0.6	91.0	68.2	9.1	45.9

Toronto Blue Jays 2019

Clayton Richard, continued

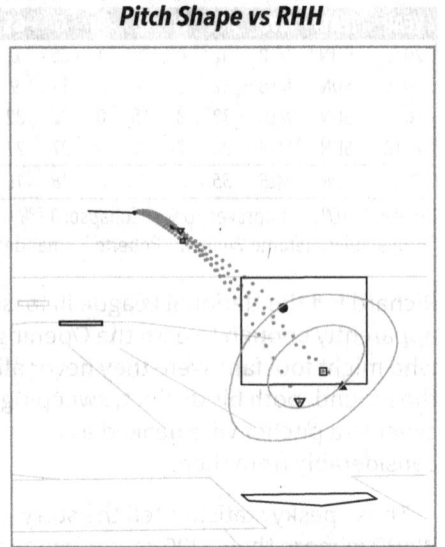

Type	Frequency	Velocity	H Movement	V Movement
● Fastball	11.0%	90.9 [95]	11.3 [79]	-19.4 [89]
□ Sinker	55.0%	90.5 [90]	15.8 [74]	-27.2 [78]
+ Cutter				
▲ Changeup	6.3%	84.6 [97]	12.4 [94]	-30.4 [91]
× Splitter				
▽ Slider	27.7%	81.3 [86]	-0.1 [79]	-39.3 [81]
◇ Curveball				
⊕ Slow Curveball				
✱ Knuckleball				
▼ Screwball				

Aaron Sanchez   RHP

Born: 07/01/92   Age: 26   Bats: R   Throws: R
Height: 6'4"   Weight: 215   Origin: Round 1, 2010 Draft (#34 overall)

YEAR	TEAM	LVL	AGE	W	L	SV	G	GS	IP	H	HR	BB/9	K/9	K	GB%	BABIP
2016	TOR	MLB	23	15	2	0	30	30	192	161	15	3.0	7.5	161	55%	.267
2017	TOR	MLB	24	1	3	0	8	8	36	42	6	5.0	6.0	24	48%	.310
2018	TOR	MLB	25	4	6	0	20	20	105	106	11	5.0	7.4	86	50%	.304
2019	TOR	MLB	26	8	9	0	24	24	136	132	16	4.0	7.2	110	49%	.288

Breakout: 20%   Improve: 52%   Collapse: 20%   Attrition: 8%   MLB: 89%
Comparables: Sonny Gray, Brandon Webb, Carlos Zambrano

Stripping Sanchez of his potential as the next Blue Jays headliner would have been unheard of three years ago, but so too would surgical fingernail removal, a blister that unspooled his fastball grip and a meager 28 starts scattered across two seasons and 141 total innings. His injury woes veered into the extreme and ridiculous in 2018 when he caught his right index finger in a falling suitcase, then lost another nine weeks to the disabled list before undergoing his second finger-related procedure in September. Though the young righty still generates above-average heat, blisters are tricky, tricky devils to tame, and it's foolish to pretend he's only one suitcase-free stretch away from an encore star-level performance in 2019.

YEAR	TEAM	LVL	AGE	WHIP	ERA	DRA	WARP	MPH	FB%	WHF	CSP
2016	TOR	MLB	23	1.17	3.00	3.77	3.5	97.5	74.5	9.2	47.7
2017	TOR	MLB	24	1.72	4.25	7.30	-0.7	96.9	76.9	6.5	44.7
2018	TOR	MLB	25	1.56	4.89	5.97	-0.8	95.9	64.5	10.5	44.9
2019	TOR	MLB	26	1.39	4.56	4.82	1.0	96.4	71.6	9.6	46.4

Toronto Blue Jays 2019

Aaron Sanchez, continued

Pitch Shape vs LHH

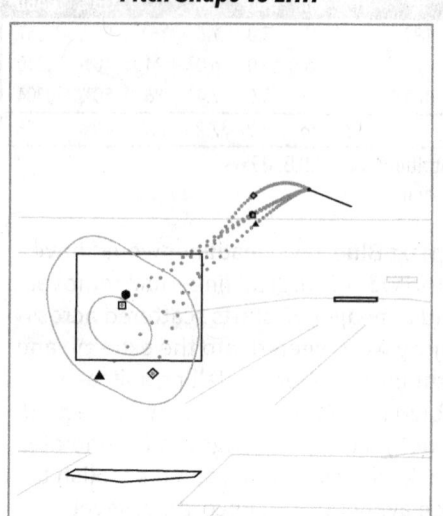

Pitch Shape vs RHH

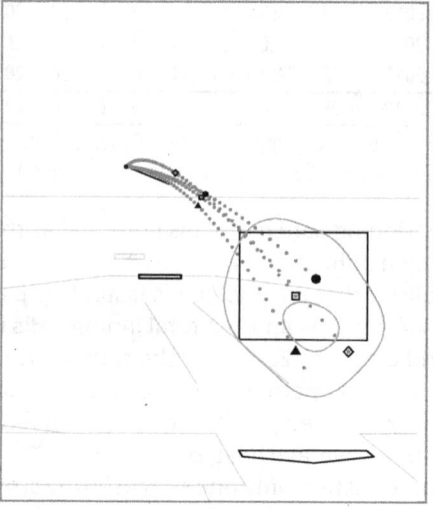

Type	Frequency	Velocity	H Movement	V Movement
● Fastball	26.6%	94.3 [106]	-11.5 [78]	-14.6 [104]
☐ Sinker	37.9%	94.2 [108]	-14.8 [82]	-17.9 [108]
+ Cutter				
▲ Changeup	23.5%	88.9 [114]	-16 [75]	-26.8 [102]
✕ Splitter				
▽ Slider				
◇ Curveball	12.0%	79.5 [104]	13.8 [125]	-51.4 [92]
⊕ Slow Curveball				
✱ Knuckleball				
▼ Screwball				

Matt Shoemaker   RHP

Born: 09/27/86   Age: 32   Bats: R   Throws: R
Height: 6'2"   Weight: 225   Origin: Undrafted Free Agent, 2008

YEAR	TEAM	LVL	AGE	W	L	SV	G	GS	IP	H	HR	BB/9	K/9	K	GB%	BABIP
2016	SLC	AAA	29	1	0	0	1	1	6	6	1	3.0	12.0	8	50%	.333
2016	ANA	MLB	29	9	13	0	27	27	160	166	18	1.7	8.0	143	42%	.315
2017	ANA	MLB	30	6	3	0	14	14	77^2	73	15	3.2	8.0	69	40%	.278
2018	ANA	MLB	31	2	2	0	7	7	31	29	3	2.9	9.6	33	44%	.313
2019	TOR	MLB	32	5	6	0	16	16	91	88	13	3.0	8.6	87	42%	.296

Breakout: 21%   Improve: 50%   Collapse: 27%   Attrition: 16%   MLB: 95%
Comparables: Chris Capuano, Brett Myers, Scott Kazmir

Both the nerve (colloquial term for audacity) and the nerve (set of axons that receive transmissions from the brain) of Shoemaker took its toll as a second surgery to repair a nerve in his elbow—and also a tendon while they were at it—shelved him for five months. Fortunately, he did get September to do some organized sports. All his pitches returned as normal, and some looked better than expected (such as his strikeout rate), so with a proper spring training and no doctors rooting around inside his arm looking for weird little things to fix, his rotation reservation should be intact.

YEAR	TEAM	LVL	AGE	WHIP	ERA	DRA	WARP	MPH	FB%	WHF	CSP
2016	SLC	AAA	29	1.33	1.50	1.86	0.2				
2016	ANA	MLB	29	1.23	3.88	4.36	1.8	94.4	49.4	13.9	47.4
2017	ANA	MLB	30	1.30	4.52	5.86	-0.2	93.9	49.5	12.4	45.6
2018	ANA	MLB	31	1.26	4.94	5.60	-0.1	93.7	47.1	13.4	46.2
2019	TOR	MLB	32	1.31	4.17	4.40	1.1	93.2	48.6	13.2	45.8

Matt Shoemaker, continued

Pitch Shape vs LHH

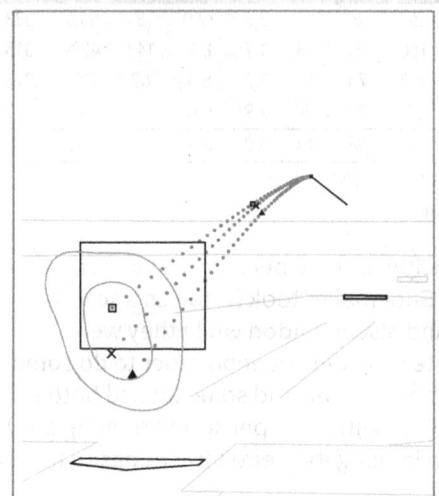

Pitch Shape vs RHH

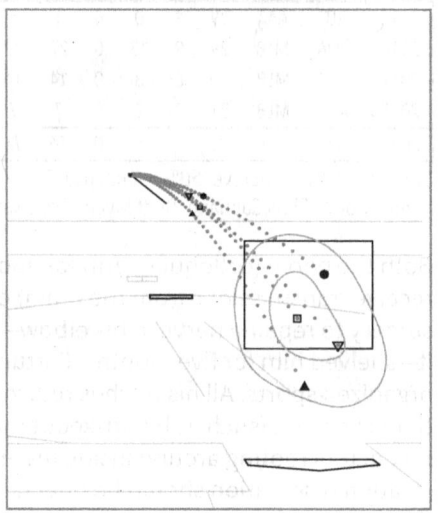

Type	Frequency	Velocity	H Movement	V Movement
● Fastball	13.0%	92 [98]	-6.7 [100]	-14.6 [104]
☐ Sinker	34.1%	91.8 [97]	-13.1 [96]	-19.7 [102]
+ Cutter				
▲ Changeup	14.6%	85.8 [102]	-8.7 [113]	-29.3 [94]
✕ Splitter	13.6%	85.6 [100]	-9.2 [96]	-29 [102]
▽ Slider	22.6%	82.8 [93]	1.9 [87]	-32.5 [102]
◇ Curveball	2.0%	78.1 [99]	8.5 [103]	-40.5 [117]
✦ Slow Curveball				
✶ Knuckleball				
▼ Screwball				

Marcus Stroman RHP

Born: 05/01/91 Age: 28 Bats: R Throws: R
Height: 5'8" Weight: 180 Origin: Round 1, 2012 Draft (#22 overall)

YEAR	TEAM	LVL	AGE	W	L	SV	G	GS	IP	H	HR	BB/9	K/9	K	GB%	BABIP
2016	TOR	MLB	25	9	10	0	32	32	204	209	21	2.4	7.3	166	62%	.309
2017	TOR	MLB	26	13	9	0	33	33	201	201	21	2.8	7.3	164	63%	.310
2018	TOR	MLB	27	4	9	0	19	19	102^1	115	9	3.2	6.8	77	64%	.326
2019	TOR	MLB	28	10	9	0	28	28	159	162	16	2.9	7.1	125	58%	.302

Breakout: 20% Improve: 45% Collapse: 25% Attrition: 5% MLB: 96%
Comparables: Johnny Cueto, Sonny Gray, Roy Halladay

The ace, the face of the franchise, the unpaid social media hype man… Stroman wears a lot of hats these days. His newest hat, that of an injured front-end starter coming off of a career year in 2017, didn't suit him quite as well as the others. Shoulder fatigue dogged him throughout the first half of the season and a nasty blister-turned-gaping wound cropped up on his right middle finger, running the rest of his campaign into the ground faster than Kathleen Wynne's re-election effort. There's no guarantee that Stroman can put his injury-riddled days behind him in 2019, but neither is there any compelling reason to believe his middling 2018 performance was anything graver than a fluke for the Cy Young finalist.

YEAR	TEAM	LVL	AGE	WHIP	ERA	DRA	WARP	MPH	FB%	WHF	CSP
2016	TOR	MLB	25	1.29	4.37	3.66	4.0	94.6	57.4	10	47.6
2017	TOR	MLB	26	1.31	3.09	4.18	3.1	94.9	62.2	10.6	46.7
2018	TOR	MLB	27	1.48	5.54	4.19	1.3	93.5	49.3	9.8	47.3
2019	TOR	MLB	28	1.36	3.99	4.18	2.3	93.9	57.4	10.3	47.5

Toronto Blue Jays 2019

Marcus Stroman, continued

Pitch Shape vs LHH

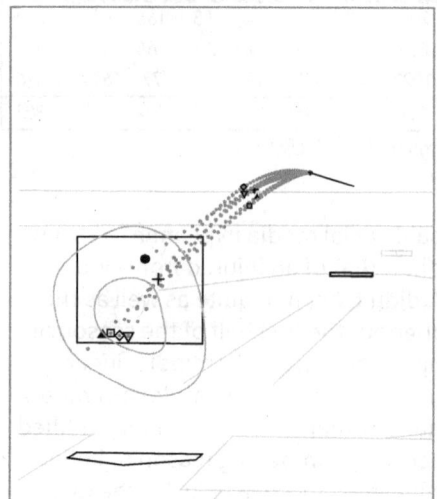

Pitch Shape vs RHH

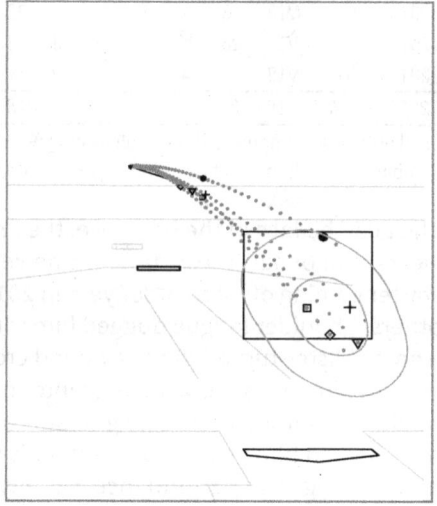

Type	Frequency	Velocity	H Movement	V Movement
● Fastball	5.4%	93.2 [102]	-3.5 [115]	-16.2 [99]
□ Sinker	43.9%	92.7 [101]	-8.6 [133]	-23.5 [90]
+ Cutter	15.5%	91 [113]	2 [101]	-23.1 [103]
▲ Changeup	4.6%	83.2 [91]	-12.3 [95]	-28.6 [96]
✕ Splitter				
▽ Slider	22.4%	86.1 [107]	9.7 [121]	-33.6 [98]
◇ Curveball	8.2%	83 [117]	12.1 [118]	-36.5 [126]
⊕ Slow Curveball				
✱ Knuckleball				
▼ Screwball				

Ryan Tepera   RHP

Born: 11/03/87   Age: 31   Bats: R   Throws: R
Height: 6'2"   Weight: 195   Origin: Round 19, 2009 Draft (#580 overall)

YEAR	TEAM	LVL	AGE	W	L	SV	G	GS	IP	H	HR	BB/9	K/9	K	GB%	BABIP
2016	BUF	AAA	28	1	2	18	37	0	45^1	33	3	3.2	9.5	48	47%	.265
2016	TOR	MLB	28	0	1	0	20	0	18^1	17	1	3.9	8.8	18	59%	.291
2017	TOR	MLB	29	7	1	2	73	0	77^2	57	7	3.6	9.4	81	43%	.260
2018	TOR	MLB	30	5	5	7	68	0	64^2	55	9	3.3	9.5	68	44%	.291
2019	TOR	MLB	31	3	3	5	56	0	59	51	7	3.9	9.1	60	44%	.286

Breakout: 24%   Improve: 40%   Collapse: 23%   Attrition: 20%   MLB: 71%
Comparables: Doug Slaten, Cory Gearrin, Will Harris

A legitimate closer option in Roberto Osuna's absence, **Ryan Tepera** was anything but tepid during his second full season in the majors. The journeyman reliever didn't blow away hitters with the same high-octane stuff of his breakout year in 2017, but continued to make subtle refinements as he chipped away at an ungainly walk rate and battled through a case of elbow inflammation.

YEAR	TEAM	LVL	AGE	WHIP	ERA	DRA	WARP	MPH	FB%	WHF	CSP
2016	BUF	AAA	28	1.08	2.58	2.62	1.2				
2016	TOR	MLB	28	1.36	2.95	4.01	0.2	97.3	53.8	14.6	42.2
2017	TOR	MLB	29	1.13	3.59	4.85	0.3	96.1	59	14.2	43.9
2018	TOR	MLB	30	1.22	3.62	4.92	0.0	96.4	61.3	14.8	43.3
2019	TOR	MLB	31	1.30	4.14	4.34	0.5	95.5	59.3	14.5	42.9

Toronto Blue Jays 2019

Ryan Tepera, continued

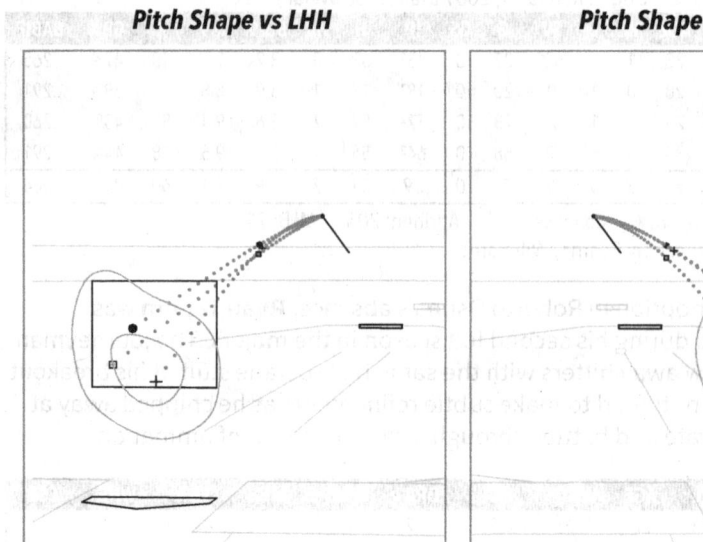

Type	Frequency	Velocity	H Movement	V Movement
● Fastball	31.5%	95.4 [109]	-6.8 [99]	-12.4 [111]
□ Sinker	29.8%	95.5 [115]	-13.3 [95]	-16 [114]
+ Cutter	32.7%	89.6 [105]	4.2 [114]	-26.2 [90]
▲ Changeup	1.7%	89.7 [117]	-12.7 [92]	-23.5 [111]
✕ Splitter				
▽ Slider	4.3%	84.1 [99]	7.5 [111]	-35.4 [93]
◇ Curveball				
✦ Slow Curveball				
✳ Knuckleball				
▼ Screwball				

Anthony Alford CF

Born: 07/20/94 Age: 24 Bats: R Throws: R
Height: 6'1" Weight: 215 Origin: Round 3, 2012 Draft (#112 overall)

YEAR	TEAM	LVL	AGE	PA	R	2B	3B	HR	RBI	BB	K	SB	CS	AVG/OBP/SLG
2016	DUN	A+	21	401	53	17	2	9	44	53	117	18	6	.236/.344/.378
2017	TOR	MLB	22	8	0	1	0	0	0	0	3	0	0	.125/.125/.250
2017	NHP	AA	22	289	41	14	0	5	24	35	45	18	3	.310/.406/.429
2018	BUF	AAA	23	417	52	22	1	5	34	30	112	17	7	.240/.312/.344
2018	TOR	MLB	23	21	3	0	0	0	1	2	9	1	0	.105/.190/.105
2019	TOR	MLB	24	141	15	6	0	3	14	9	40	4	1	.219/.279/.336

Breakout: 11%   Improve: 22%   Collapse: 1%   Attrition: 16%   MLB: 30%
Comparables: Reymond Fuentes, Drew Stubbs, Brian Goodwin

"Exceptional when healthy" is a maxim so liberally applied as to be rendered meaningless. In Alford's case, however, it just so happens to be true. The former Southern Miss defensive back converted to high-speed outfielder in 2012 and continues to profile well across the board, from his advanced technique and above-average bat speed at the plate to his natural instincts on the grass. While he has yet to make a real impact for the Blue Jays on a big-league level, he's also seen more than his fair share of injuries in recent years, from a concussion in 2016 to a cracked hamate bone in 2017 to a nagging hamstring issue in 2018. Expect the club to keep a hawk-like watch over the two-way talent until he's deemed healthy enough for a prolonged stint in the majors.

YEAR	TEAM	LVL	AGE	PA	DRC+	VORP	BABIP	BRR	FRAA	WARP
2016	DUN	A+	21	401	107	15.0	.327	2.3	CF(84): 2.6, LF(6): 1.7	1.3
2017	TOR	MLB	22	8	65	-0.8	.200	0.0	LF(3): -0.2, RF(2): 0.0	0.0
2017	NHP	AA	22	289	135	22.0	.360	2.5	CF(35): 5.1, LF(13): 1.0	2.1
2018	BUF	AAA	23	417	96	9.0	.327	4.5	CF(43): 2.9, LF(31): -1.7	0.8
2018	TOR	MLB	23	21	75	-0.9	.200	0.7	LF(7): 0.2, RF(3): -0.1	0.1
2019	TOR	MLB	24	141	71	0.2	.300	0.3	CF 1, LF 0	0.1

Toronto Blue Jays 2019

Bo Bichette SS
Born: 03/05/98   Age: 21   Bats: R   Throws: R
Height: 6'0"   Weight: 200   Origin: Round 2, 2016 Draft (#66 overall)

YEAR	TEAM	LVL	AGE	PA	R	2B	3B	HR	RBI	BB	K	SB	CS	AVG/OBP/SLG
2016	BLJ	RK	18	91	21	9	2	4	36	6	17	3	0	.427/.451/.732
2017	LNS	A	19	317	60	32	3	10	51	28	55	12	3	.384/.448/.623
2017	DUN	A+	19	182	28	9	1	4	23	14	26	10	4	.323/.379/.463
2018	NHP	AA	20	595	95	43	7	11	74	48	101	32	11	.286/.343/.453
2019	TOR	MLB	21	251	32	15	2	7	26	11	61	7	2	.249/.280/.416

Breakout: 21%   Improve: 38%   Collapse: 10%   Attrition: 28%   MLB: 51%
Comparables: Franklin Barreto, Addison Russell, Alen Hanson

It's the bane of every younger sibling's existence to have their accomplishments and talents juxtaposed against those of their older siblings. Granted, Bichette bears no blood relation to fellow top prospect and Hall of Fame progeny Vladimir Guerrero Jr. (nor is he technically the younger of the two), but given his current status as the no. 2 talent in Toronto's system, comparisons are as frequent and inevitable as they are unwarranted. The six-foot, 200-pound shortstop is no Niles Crane to a decorated, pompous Frasier, however—he stands tall in his own right with a bat that plays for both average and power and an aggressive approach at the plate that has overwhelmed opponents at every level so far. He's still fairly limited at his natural position, but the glove may eventually skew above-average while he rises to meet a lofty offensive ceiling.

YEAR	TEAM	LVL	AGE	PA	DRC+	VORP	BABIP	BRR	FRAA	WARP
2016	BLJ	RK	18	91	264	19.5	.484	-0.4	SS(16): 1.7, 2B(6): 0.3	1.5
2017	LNS	A	19	317	209	48.4	.452	3.0	SS(51): 0.2, 2B(14): 0.3	5.0
2017	DUN	A+	19	182	146	12.5	.360	-0.2	SS(35): -0.3	1.1
2018	NHP	AA	20	595	125	40.6	.331	3.2	SS(116): -4.0, 2B(9): 0.6	3.1
2019	TOR	MLB	21	251	83	5.2	.302	0.6	SS 0, 2B 0	0.6

Cavan Biggio INF

Born: 04/11/95   Age: 24   Bats: L   Throws: R
Height: 6'1"   Weight: 203   Origin: Round 5, 2016 Draft (#162 overall)

YEAR	TEAM	LVL	AGE	PA	R	2B	3B	HR	RBI	BB	K	SB	CS	AVG/OBP/SLG
2016	VAN	A-	21	238	24	11	3	0	21	29	28	9	3	.282/.382/.366
2016	LNS	A	21	42	3	1	0	0	5	4	7	2	0	.222/.310/.250
2017	DUN	A+	22	556	75	17	5	11	60	74	140	11	7	.233/.342/.363
2018	NHP	AA	23	563	80	23	5	26	99	100	148	20	8	.252/.388/.499
2019	TOR	MLB	24	251	32	7	1	9	26	30	73	4	2	.182/.282/.347

Breakout: 8%   Improve: 19%   Collapse: 2%   Attrition: 22%   MLB: 32%
Comparables: Drew Robinson, Alex Blandino, Darnell Sweeney

Clawing one's way out from under the shadow of a successful parent—one whose legacy is enshrined in Cooperstown, no less—is a formidable task independent of profession or person. While Biggio hasn't yet carved a clear path to the majors like Vladimir Guerrero Jr. and Bo Bichette, such comparisons minimize the pronounced effect he cast during his first full year as a 26-homer, 20-stolen base threat in Double-A ball. His defense has yet to mature alongside his bat, particularly at the keystone, but the power is legitimate, the advanced approach at the plate even more appealing, and the positional versatility a promising sign of things to come.

YEAR	TEAM	LVL	AGE	PA	DRC+	VORP	BABIP	BRR	FRAA	WARP
2016	VAN	A-	21	238	128	13.1	.324	-0.4	2B(49): -3.0	0.0
2016	LNS	A	21	42	84	-0.3	.267	-0.8	2B(9): 0.6	-0.1
2017	DUN	A+	22	556	95	10.2	.304	1.1	2B(116): 6.4, 3B(6): -0.4	0.8
2018	NHP	AA	23	563	135	44.8	.307	3.6	2B(68): 1.5, 3B(34): -1.1	3.5
2019	TOR	MLB	24	251	73	-1.0	.221	0.2	2B 1, 3B -1	-0.1

Toronto Blue Jays 2019

Vladimir Guerrero Jr. 3B

Born: 03/16/99   Age: 20   Bats: R   Throws: R
Height: 6'1"   Weight: 200   Origin: International Free Agent, 2015

YEAR	TEAM	LVL	AGE	PA	R	2B	3B	HR	RBI	BB	K	SB	CS	AVG/OBP/SLG
2016	BLU	RK	17	276	32	12	3	8	46	33	35	15	5	.271/.359/.449
2017	LNS	A	18	318	53	21	1	7	45	40	34	6	2	.316/.409/.480
2017	DUN	A+	18	209	31	7	1	6	31	36	28	2	2	.333/.450/.494
2018	NHP	AA	19	266	48	19	1	14	60	21	27	3	3	.402/.449/.671
2018	BUF	AAA	19	128	15	7	0	6	16	15	10	0	0	.336/.414/.564
2019	TOR	MLB	20	455	63	24	1	21	67	37	70	1	1	.310/.370/.527

Breakout: 24%   Improve: 39%   Collapse: 1%   Attrition: 6%   MLB: 41%
Comparables: Jason Heyward, Mike Trout, Jurickson Profar

In an industry that churns up and spits out maybe a dozen elite prospects in a calendar year, if that, it's a badge of pride to be able to say that you noticed when the Next Big Thing first appeared on the horizon. For scouts of decades past, that kind of talent manifested in younger versions of Ken Griffey, Jr., Alex Rodriguez, Miguel Cabrera, Mike Trout and Bryce Harper. For those combing through the back fields and minor league networks of today's pro ball landscape, it's currently packaged in the form of Vladimir Guerrero, Jr.

Guerrero may have grown up in his father's journey to Cooperstown, but he stepped into the sunlight at an early age with the kind of power-driven bat and top prospect potential that sent Tom Tsuchiya scrambling for fresh clay and a new bronze mold. "Powerful" doesn't begin to describe the teenager's utter lack of discrimination between pitches as he anticipates and reverses triple-digit heaters, dirt-digging sliders and arching curveballs out of the park, leaving outfielders hung out to dry like washed-up superheroes clinging to the tops of the fences.

After tunneling his way through the lower levels of the Blue Jays' system, Guerrero turned his bat on Double- and Triple-A pitchers with similar ferocity. His staggering on-base clip regressed slightly as he moved up the ranks, an anticipated result of facing higher-caliber opponents, but the underlying ability to hit for power and average still rings true. Although his glove is never going to catch up with his hit tool, he has the build and instincts for the hot corner and will remain a fixture there while he rewrites the very definition of a 'pure hitter' for the next generation.

YEAR	TEAM	LVL	AGE	PA	DRC+	VORP	BABIP	BRR	FRAA	WARP
2016	BLU	RK	17	276	134	19.2	.283	1.5	3B(50): -10.7	-0.2
2017	LNS	A	18	318	172	26.9	.336	0.8	3B(61): -2.6	2.9
2017	DUN	A+	18	209	182	17.1	.365	-2.4	3B(41): -1.5	1.5
2018	NHP	AA	19	266	192	37.4	.402	-2.9	3B(53): 1.0	2.9
2018	BUF	AAA	19	128	185	11.5	.323	-4.8	3B(25): 4.3	1.4
2019	TOR	MLB	20	455	137	31.1	.328	-1.0	3B 0	3.1

Toronto Blue Jays 2019

Reese McGuire   C
Born: 03/02/95   Age: 24   Bats: L   Throws: R
Height: 5'11"   Weight: 215   Origin: Round 1, 2013 Draft (#14 overall)

YEAR	TEAM	LVL	AGE	PA	R	2B	3B	HR	RBI	BB	K	SB	CS	AVG/OBP/SLG
2016	ALT	AA	21	304	29	16	2	1	37	29	26	4	4	.259/.337/.346
2016	NHP	AA	21	61	5	2	0	0	5	7	8	2	2	.226/.328/.264
2017	NHP	AA	22	136	19	5	1	6	20	16	19	2	1	.278/.366/.496
2018	BUF	AAA	23	369	31	9	2	7	37	33	77	3	2	.233/.312/.339
2018	TOR	MLB	23	33	5	3	0	2	4	2	9	1	0	.290/.333/.581
2019	TOR	MLB	24	58	6	2	0	2	6	4	12	0	0	.231/.298/.385

Breakout: 10%   Improve: 30%   Collapse: 0%   Attrition: 21%   MLB: 44%
Comparables: Austin Barnes, Mitch Garver, J.T. Realmuto

The Blue Jays are looking to develop their next franchise backstop as the Russell Martin era winds down, and the defense-driven McGuire proved a key platoon candidate when rosters expanded last fall. While his bat doesn't possess Martin's maturation or Danny Jansen's pop, the 2013 first-rounder acquitted himself well during a handful of introductory at-bats in Toronto and may yet pose more than a passing threat in the batter's box. With a plus arm and a demonstrated ability to control the running game, however, the lefty's above-average defense still profiles as his best asset—anything else is simply the cherry on top.

YEAR	TEAM	P. COUNT	FRM RUNS	BLK RUNS	THRW RUNS	TOT RUNS
2017	NHP	4206	4.4	0.1	0.0	4.6
2018	BUF	9552	15.4	0.2	0.3	15.9
2018	TOR	1355	0.4	0.5	-0.1	1.0
2019	TOR	2187	0.8	0.0	0.0	0.8

YEAR	TEAM	LVL	AGE	PA	DRC+	VORP	BABIP	BRR	FRAA	WARP
2016	ALT	AA	21	304	93	8.5	.282	-1.8	C(73): 0.5	0.5
2016	NHP	AA	21	61	97	-0.2	.267	0.7	C(13): -0.1	0.2
2017	NHP	AA	22	136	138	11.3	.283	-1.9	C(34): 5.0	1.3
2018	BUF	AAA	23	369	94	8.7	.281	1.6	C(73): 15.0	2.4
2018	TOR	MLB	23	33	95	3.3	.350	0.3	C(11): 0.7	0.2
2019	TOR	MLB	24	58	74	0.8	.255	-0.1	C 0	0.1

Max Pentecost   C

Born: 03/10/93   Age: 26   Bats: R   Throws: R
Height: 6'2"   Weight: 191   Origin: Round 1, 2014 Draft (#11 overall)

YEAR	TEAM	LVL	AGE	PA	R	2B	3B	HR	RBI	BB	K	SB	CS	AVG/OBP/SLG
2016	LNS	A	23	267	36	15	3	7	34	21	51	4	2	.314/.375/.490
2016	DUN	A+	23	52	6	2	0	3	7	3	17	1	1	.245/.288/.469
2017	DUN	A+	24	314	34	14	2	9	54	23	62	0	1	.276/.332/.434
2018	NHP	AA	25	368	40	17	2	10	52	15	89	1	0	.253/.283/.401
2019	TOR	MLB	26	251	21	9	1	8	28	7	71	0	0	.211/.233/.350

Breakout: 6%   Improve: 11%   Collapse: 2%   Attrition: 17%   MLB: 21%
Comparables: John Hester, Craig Tatum, Lucas May

YEAR	TEAM	P. COUNT	FRM RUNS	BLK RUNS	THRW RUNS	TOT RUNS
2018	NHP	10574	-13.2	0.1	1.7	-10.3
2019	TOR	8816	-14.4	-0.4	0.3	-14.5

Whispers of Pentecost's prowess behind the plate began to sound more like fairy tale lore than fact after the young backstop was cursed with repeated shoulder injuries following his first-round selection in the 2014 draft. When he was finally cleared to monitor the dish in Double-A—the result of a painstaking rehab process or the benevolence of a wish-granting genie, we'll never know—he advanced his hero's journey with half a season's worth of starts, a 40 percent caught stealing rate, and a refined power stroke at the plate. Moving forward, consistency will be key, but don't write him off as a lost cause just yet.

YEAR	TEAM	LVL	AGE	PA	DRC+	VORP	BABIP	BRR	FRAA	WARP
2016	LNS	A	23	267	145	19.0	.370	1.5		1.4
2016	DUN	A+	23	52	90	0.3	.310	-0.2		-0.1
2017	DUN	A+	24	314	126	10.2	.323	-1.5	1B(22): 0.8, C(19): -0.3	0.6
2018	NHP	AA	25	368	80	11.9	.306	1.6	C(77): -10.0	-0.6
2019	TOR	MLB	26	251	54	-3.0	.262	-0.4	C -14	-1.8

Dalton Pompey OF

Born: 12/11/92 Age: 26 Bats: B Throws: R
Height: 6'2" Weight: 195 Origin: Round 16, 2010 Draft (#486 overall)

YEAR	TEAM	LVL	AGE	PA	R	2B	3B	HR	RBI	BB	K	SB	CS	AVG/OBP/SLG
2016	BUF	AAA	23	383	48	14	1	4	28	40	72	18	7	.270/.349/.353
2016	TOR	MLB	23	2	3	0	0	0	0	0	1	2	1	.000/.000/.000
2018	TOR	MLB	25	11	0	0	0	0	0	1	6	0	0	.200/.273/.200
2018	BUF	AAA	25	168	22	8	0	4	17	14	41	8	2	.255/.325/.393
2019	TOR	MLB	26	251	31	9	1	6	22	18	64	8	3	.224/.289/.348

Breakout: 5% Improve: 23% Collapse: 11% Attrition: 22% MLB: 50%
Comparables: Thomas Neal, Dave Sappelt, Brandon Guyer

"It is not the last drop that empties the water-clock," Seneca cautioned Lucilius, "but all that which previously has flowed out; similarly, the final hour when we cease to exist does not of itself bring death; it merely of itself completes the death process." So, too, is the way of a decaying career, as Pompey discovered after a string of injury-laden seasons extended to a wrist sprain in early March and a partial UCL tear in his left thumb by June. That fatal, unbearable drop emptied Pompey's clock in August, when Triple-A manager Bobby Meacham made a seemingly innocuous decision to pinch-hit for the former top prospect in the second inning of a split doubleheader. Pompey blew up at Meacham, was swiftly suspended without pay, and finished out the year batting .167 over his last dozen games, further away from a major-league gig than ever before.

YEAR	TEAM	LVL	AGE	PA	DRC+	VORP	BABIP	BRR	FRAA	WARP
2016	BUF	AAA	23	383	107	13.9	.331	5.2	CF(67): -0.6, LF(24): -0.3	1.4
2016	TOR	MLB	23	2	82	-0.4	.000	0.1	LF(2): -0.1	0.0
2018	TOR	MLB	25	11	69	-0.9	.500	0.1	LF(3): -0.3	0.0
2018	BUF	AAA	25	168	106	8.3	.317	1.7	RF(18): -3.0, LF(14): -2.3	-0.3
2019	TOR	MLB	26	251	75	0.5	.284	0.4	LF 0, RF -2	-0.2

Forrest Wall CF

Born: 11/20/95   Age: 23   Bats: L   Throws: R
Height: 6'0"   Weight: 176   Origin: Round 1, 2014 Draft (#35 overall)

YEAR	TEAM	LVL	AGE	PA	R	2B	3B	HR	RBI	BB	K	SB	CS	AVG/OBP/SLG
2016	MOD	A+	20	521	57	16	4	6	56	41	97	22	11	.264/.329/.355
2017	LNC	A+	21	98	17	4	1	3	16	9	16	5	3	.299/.361/.471
2018	LNC	A+	22	230	43	11	5	3	19	23	47	20	8	.305/.382/.453
2018	HFD	AA	22	190	27	6	1	6	12	17	42	8	3	.206/.289/.359
2018	NHP	AA	22	147	19	7	2	1	13	13	46	10	3	.271/.354/.380
2019	TOR	MLB	23	251	30	7	2	6	21	13	68	8	3	.205/.254/.331

Breakout: 2%   Improve: 5%   Collapse: 0%   Attrition: 5%   MLB: 6%
Comparables: Blake Tekotte, Jacob May, Andrew Stevenson

A year after he saw his season derailed by a freak shoulder dislocation, Wall's major league future remains as unpredictable and full of potential as an episode of, well, *The Wall*. The former 35th overall pick headlined a package deal for reliever Seung-hwan Oh in July and used his plus speed to both steal nearly 40 bases across two levels and take circuitous routes to fly balls. It seems unlikely that the Blue Jays would risk everything to roll the dice (er, "triple up") on a fringe-average fourth outfielder, but if there's any lesson to be gleaned from watching sweaty-palmed contestants attempt to manipulate the random workings of a four-foot pegboard, it's this: Sometimes the unlikeliest gamble reaps the biggest dividends.

YEAR	TEAM	LVL	AGE	PA	DRC+	VORP	BABIP	BRR	FRAA	WARP
2016	MOD	A+	20	521	80	18.2	.319	0.6	2B(117): -4.5	-1.2
2017	LNC	A+	21	98	124	5.9	.333	2.4	CF(17): 0.5, LF(2): -0.4	0.5
2018	LNC	A+	22	230	130	14.5	.386	1.4	CF(39): -11.1, LF(1): 0.7	-0.2
2018	HFD	AA	22	190	80	0.9	.238	2.3	CF(26): -1.7, LF(18): 4.5	0.4
2018	NHP	AA	22	147	83	3.5	.410	-0.6	CF(34): -6.5	-0.8
2019	TOR	MLB	23	251	58	-2.7	.258	0.8	CF -5, LF 1	-0.8

Toronto Blue Jays 2019

Justin Maese   RHP
Born: 10/24/96   Age: 22   Bats: R   Throws: R
Height: 6'3"   Weight: 190   Origin: Round 3, 2015 Draft (#91 overall)

YEAR	TEAM	LVL	AGE	W	L	SV	G	GS	IP	H	HR	BB/9	K/9	K	GB%	BABIP
2016	VAN	A-	19	2	2	0	5	5	26^1	20	1	0.3	6.8	20	68%	.241
2016	LNS	A	19	2	4	0	10	10	56^1	59	2	2.2	7.0	44	57%	.331
2017	LNS	A	20	5	3	0	12	12	70^2	78	3	3.3	7.6	60	55%	.341
2019	TOR	MLB	22	2	3	0	6	6	33^1	39	5	3.5	6.1	22	48%	.313

Breakout: 2%   Improve: 3%   Collapse: 0%   Attrition: 2%   MLB: 3%
Comparables: Myles Jaye, Joely Rodriguez, Jace Fry

The only thing worse than watching a promising young pitcher tough his way through an injury-shortened season is watching him do it twice. The shoulder impingement that dogged Maese in 2017 lingered well into the late spring of 2018, forcing the right-hander and his wicked mid-90s fastball to forego a reservation in High-A Dunedin's rotation, and erased any likelihood that he might soon crack the upper echelon of the club's prospect hierarchy.

YEAR	TEAM	LVL	AGE	WHIP	ERA	DRA	WARP	MPH	FB%	WHF	CSP
2016	VAN	A-	19	0.80	2.05	2.58	0.8				
2016	LNS	A	19	1.30	3.36	5.33	-0.2				
2017	LNS	A	20	1.47	4.84	5.22	0.1				
2019	TOR	MLB	22	1.55	5.21	5.36	0.0				

Eric Pardinho   RHP
Born: 01/05/01   Age: 18   Bats: R   Throws: R
Height: 5'10"   Weight: 155   Origin: International Free Agent, 2018

YEAR	TEAM	LVL	AGE	W	L	SV	G	GS	IP	H	HR	BB/9	K/9	K	GB%	BABIP
2018	BLU	RK	17	4	3	0	11	11	50	37	5	2.9	11.5	64	47%	.274
2019	TOR	MLB	18	1	3	0	7	7	32^1	35	6	5.3	8.2	29	44%	.310

Comparables: Mike Soroka, Martin Perez, Roberto Osuna

If Pardinho had been born in the United States, rather than his native Brazil, he'd have spent the start of last summer going to junior prom, making final decisions on college programs and playing in a bunch of showcases to prepare for the 2019 Draft. Instead, the 17-year-old was one of the best pitchers in the Appy League—and that's without even adjusting for age. During his stateside debut, the right-hander showed off a strong and balanced four-pitch mix, led by a mid-90s fastball and a curve that punished hitters 4-5 years his senior. A full-season debut awaits in 2019, while the rest of his peers hire "advisors," participate in final workouts and obsess over mock draft positioning.

YEAR	TEAM	LVL	AGE	WHIP	ERA	DRA	WARP	MPH	FB%	WHF	CSP
2018	BLU	RK	17	1.06	2.88	3.62	1.3				
2019	TOR	MLB	18	1.68	5.92	6.12	-0.2				

David Paulino RHP

Born: 02/06/94   Age: 25   Bats: R   Throws: R
Height: 6'7"   Weight: 222   Origin: International Free Agent, 2010

YEAR	TEAM	LVL	AGE	W	L	SV	G	GS	IP	H	HR	BB/9	K/9	K	GB%	BABIP
2016	AST	RK	22	0	0	0	3	3	12	9	0	1.5	10.5	14	75%	.281
2016	CCH	AA	22	5	2	1	14	9	64	47	3	1.5	10.1	72	40%	.280
2016	FRE	AAA	22	0	2	0	3	3	14	16	1	3.9	12.9	20	45%	.385
2016	HOU	MLB	22	0	1	0	3	1	7	6	0	3.9	2.6	2	44%	.261
2017	FRE	AAA	23	0	1	0	3	3	14	11	3	5.8	8.4	13	28%	.216
2017	HOU	MLB	23	2	0	0	6	6	29	36	8	2.2	10.6	34	33%	.359
2018	FRE	AAA	24	0	0	0	4	4	18	16	3	2.5	11.5	23	46%	.302
2018	TOR	MLB	24	1	0	0	7	0	6^2	6	1	2.7	8.1	6	50%	.263
2019	TOR	MLB	25	3	3	0	51	0	53^2	45	5	3.4	9.7	58	42%	.288

Breakout: 17%   Improve: 48%   Collapse: 21%   Attrition: 29%   MLB: 84%
Comparables: Jonathan Papelbon, Bud Norris, Brandon Workman

How quickly the mighty fall. Once an intriguing starter option, Paulino cracked the Astros' top ten list in 2016 and 2017, but one undisclosed Double-A spat, bone spur removal surgery, 80-game steroid-driven suspension and season-compromising shoulder injury later, he found himself reassigned as September bullpen depth for the non-contending Blue Jays. He still has the raw stuff that inspired the Astros to take a flier on him several years ago, but the long injury history and middling major-league results will continue to raise some eyebrows until he can prove himself healthy once again.

YEAR	TEAM	LVL	AGE	WHIP	ERA	DRA	WARP	MPH	FB%	WHF	CSP
2016	AST	RK	22	0.92	0.75	2.53	0.4				
2016	CCH	AA	22	0.91	1.83	2.31	2.1				
2016	FRE	AAA	22	1.57	3.86	2.66	0.4				
2016	HOU	MLB	22	1.29	5.14	7.55	-0.2	94.8	52.4	6.4	50.4
2017	FRE	AAA	23	1.43	4.50	5.05	0.1				
2017	HOU	MLB	23	1.48	6.52	5.45	0.0	94.0	46	11.6	48.6
2018	FRE	AAA	24	1.17	5.50	2.99	0.5				
2018	TOR	MLB	24	1.20	1.35	5.14	0.0	94.3	42.2	10.2	44.3
2019	TOR	MLB	25	1.22	3.44	3.75	0.9	93.9	47.1	10.9	48.4

Nate Pearson   RHP

Born: 08/20/96   Age: 22   Bats: R   Throws: R
Height: 6'6"   Weight: 245   Origin: Round 1, 2017 Draft (#28 overall)

YEAR	TEAM	LVL	AGE	W	L	SV	G	GS	IP	H	HR	BB/9	K/9	K	GB%	BABIP
2017	VAN	A-	20	0	0	0	7	7	19	6	0	2.4	11.4	24	40%	.158
2019	TOR	MLB	22	2	4	0	9	9	33	38	8	3.9	7.5	28	38%	.308

Breakout: 0%   Improve: 1%   Collapse: 0%   Attrition: 1%   MLB: 1%
Comparables: Elvis Araujo, Braden Shipley, Austin Voth

Pearson's runway proved shorter than expected when he collided with a nasty comebacker in his season debut and lost the year to a fractured forearm. He landed a few of his signature triple-digit pitches in the Arizona Fall League, however, and given good health, should be ready for departure again soon. Of course, the screw in his pitching elbow from surgery while in high school, among other things, will make it more difficult to him to pass through security unabated. When he's right, he pairs the pure 80-grade heat with a Syndergaardian slider that is thrown faster than most four-seamers that currently occupy the Blue Jays rotation and both a curveball and change that could get to at least average pitches in time. It's truly a profile that can give hitters a lot of turbulence at the plate. If he can overcome the risk and stay upright on a mound for the majority of 2019, well, the sky is the limit.

YEAR	TEAM	LVL	AGE	WHIP	ERA	DRA	WARP	MPH	FB%	WHF	CSP
2017	VAN	A-	20	0.58	0.95	4.39	0.2				
2019	TOR	MLB	22	1.59	6.17	6.39	-0.3				

Toronto Blue Jays 2019

LINEOUTS

Hitters

HITTER	POS	TEAM	LVL	AGE	PA	R	2B	3B	HR	RBI	BB	K	SB	CS	AVG/OBP/SLG	DRC+	WARP
Ronny Brito	SS	OGD	Rk	19	244	37	11	0	11	52	21	74	1	6	.288/.352/.489	107	0.6
Griffin Conine	RF	VAN	A–	20	230	24	14	2	7	30	19	63	5	0	.238/.309/.427	93	0.4
Jonathan Davis	OF	NHP	AA	26	358	68	22	3	5	33	35	53	19	3	.302/.388/.443	136	3.1
	OF	BUF	AAA	26	202	26	7	2	5	23	12	41	7	1	.249/.308/.389	92	0.2
	OF	TOR	MLB	26	27	3	1	0	0	0	1	6	3	0	.200/.259/.240	80	0.2
Jordan Groshans	SS	BLJ	Rk	18	159	17	12	0	4	39	13	29	0	0	.331/.390/.500	148	0.6
	SS	BLU	Rk	18	48	4	1	0	1	4	2	8	0	0	.182/.229/.273	34	-0.1
Miguel Hiraldo	3B	DBL	Rk	17	239	41	18	3	2	33	23	30	15	6	.313/.381/.453	170	2.8
	3B	BLJ	Rk	17	40	3	4	0	0	3	1	12	3	0	.231/.250/.333	49	-0.3
Luke Maile	C	TOR	MLB	27	231	22	13	1	3	27	25	67	2	0	.248/.333/.366	85	1.7
Kevin Smith	SS	LNS	A	21	204	36	23	4	7	44	17	33	12	1	.355/.407/.639	190	3.2
	SS	DUN	A+	21	371	57	8	2	18	49	23	88	17	5	.274/.332/.468	125	3.0
Eric Sogard	2B	MIL	MLB	32	113	7	3	0	0	2	12	23	3	0	.134/.241/.165	72	0.1
	2B	CSP	AAA	32	101	10	4	0	0	11	10	16	0	1	.225/.297/.270	62	0.2
Logan Warmoth	SS	DUN	A+	22	322	31	13	2	1	28	30	69	9	0	.248/.322/.319	97	1.3

Signed for a cool $2 million out of the Dominican in 2015, **Ronny Brito** drove in eight runs in a July game for the Ogden Raptors. For all you math people out there, that comes out to a quarter mil per RBI. ⓧ "Mr. Blue Jay" may not have the satisfying alliterative appeal of "Mr. Marlin," but that's okay—second-rounder **Griffin Conine** still has plenty of time to carve out his own legacy in Toronto. For this budding outfielder, that'll require some fine-tuning of the strong defensive instincts and power-driven (if overreaching) swing he already brings to the table. ⓧ Center fielder **Jonathan Davis** is a solid up-the-middle defender, but he's given little reason to think that he'll hit enough to be anything more than a spare part. ⓧ A burly first-round draft pick with raw power in spades, the only question **Jordan Groshans** has yet to answer is that of his glove. He has the experience to stick at short and the build and athleticism to become a fixture at third base. ⓧ As unlooked-for and thrilling as a summer fling, **Miguel Hiraldo** enchanted the Blue Jays with a fresh burst of power in the Dominican Summer League. Although he has yet to settle down at any one defensive position, his quick hands and dynamic swing lead some to believe he has the right stuff to go the distance. ⓧ The bar is set higher than usual for **Luke Maile**, who projects as the team's fourth-best catcher in a stacked farm system. Following a career-best year at the plate, the continued lack of opportunity behind the dish is enough to make anyone go postal. ⓧ Top-shelf international prospect **Orelvis Martinez** continues to draw promising comparisons to Adrian Beltre. Is he also a Hall of Famer in-the-making? Unlikely. Could it be the 17-year-old is a sluggish baserunner who packs a punch at the plate, swapped his right arm for a cannon and possesses the athleticism to pivot between short and third base despite lacking a path forward in an already-crowded infield? Ah, there it is. Ⓥ A true bargain-bin find if ever there was one, former fourth-round pick **Kevin Smith** continued to reap dividends for the Blue Jays following an explosive 25-homer, 29-stolen base campaign across multiple levels of A-ball. Ⓥ Up next on *America's Got Talent*, **Eric Sogard** spun a .263/.404/.368 August 2017 into $2.4 million. With these monetary skills, rumor has it President Trump might nominate this shortstop to the Federal Reserve Board. Ⓥ Frequent injuries compromised a highly-anticipated encore from standout shortstop **Logan Warmoth** during his first foray into High-A ball. His ability to touch bat to ball on a regular basis is as impressive as it is capable of distracting from a conspicuous lack of speed and power, but he'll get another opportunity to wipe the slate clean in 2019.

Pitchers

PITCHER	TEAM	LVL	AGE	W	L	SV	G	GS	IP	H	HR	BB/9	K/9	K	GB%	WHIP	ERA	DRA	WARP
Felipe Castaneda	BLU	Rk	18	2	1	0	10	10	37^2	41	5	6.7	6.9	29	45%	1.83	6.69	4.91	0.5
Yennsy Diaz	LNS	A	21	5	1	0	9	9	47^2	22	4	4.7	7.9	42	40%	0.99	2.08	6.23	-0.6
	DUN	A+	21	5	4	0	18	16	99^2	91	5	2.5	7.5	83	41%	1.19	3.52	3.31	2.3
Justin Dillon	DUN	A+	24	0	3	0	6	4	22^1	23	5	3.2	6.9	17	55%	1.39	4.43	6.70	-0.4
	BUF	AAA	24	2	1	1	4	3	22^2	10	2	0.8	7.5	19	33%	0.53	0.79	3.95	0.4
	NHP	AA	24	2	4	0	14	7	50	60	6	4.0	4.0	22	36%	1.64	6.84	4.94	0.2
Javy Guerra	NWO	AAA	32	3	0	5	12	0	16^2	9	0	1.6	13.0	24	61%	0.72	0.00	2.15	0.6
	MIA	MLB	32	1	1	1	32	0	35^2	42	4	3.0	7.6	30	45%	1.51	5.55	5.02	0.0
Zachary Jackson	NHP	AA	23	2	3	2	43	0	62	29	2	7.4	10.9	75	36%	1.29	2.47	3.26	1.2
Patrick Murphy	NHP	AA	23	0	0	0	1	1	6	4	0	4.5	9.0	6	56%	1.17	3.00	2.42	0.2
	DUN	A+	23	10	5	0	26	26	146^2	126	5	3.1	8.3	135	60%	1.20	2.64	5.28	0.1
Hector Perez	BCA	A+	22	3	3	2	17	11	72^2	50	5	5.0	10.3	83	48%	1.24	3.84	3.28	1.7
	CCH	AA	22	0	1	0	4	2	16^2	12	0	4.3	9.7	18	49%	1.20	3.24	3.20	0.4
	NHP	AA	22	0	1	0	6	5	25^2	17	1	5.6	11.2	32	37%	1.29	3.86	4.07	0.4
Trent Thornton	FRE	AAA	24	9	8	0	24	22	124^1	118	13	2.2	8.8	122	42%	1.20	4.42	3.81	2.4
Jacob Waguespack	REA	AA	24	1	1	0	7	7	29^1	31	0	4.9	9.5	31	59%	1.60	3.99	4.51	0.3
	LEH	AAA	24	3	5	1	14	8	53^1	54	4	3.4	8.1	48	52%	1.39	5.06	4.12	0.8
	BUF	AAA	24	2	4	0	7	6	39^1	47	3	2.3	7.6	33	54%	1.45	5.03	4.26	0.5
T.J. Zeuch	DUN	A+	22	3	3	0	6	6	36^1	34	4	2.2	5.9	24	63%	1.18	3.47	5.91	-0.2
	NHP	AA	22	9	5	0	21	21	120	120	7	2.3	6.1	81	56%	1.26	3.08	4.02	1.8

A bonafide changeup may be potent enough to slay low-level hitters, but **Felipe Castaneda** and his mythic pitch will never get the opportunity to square off against major league beasts if he continues to neglect the other two weapons in his arsenal: an underwhelming heater and the rough draft of a breaking ball.

ⓑ The Jays added **Yennsy Diaz** to the 40-man roster in November, and while his size may imply a move to the bullpen, his improved control in the Florida State League keeps the dream of a backend starter alive for another year. ⓑ A bad season split between High-A and Double-A being broken up by complete domination in Triple-A feels like a script error, but **Justin Dillon** basically lived a Buffalo Wild Wings commercial for a few weeks in May minus the wings. ⓑ The two days **Oliver Drake** spent in Toronto were the asymptote of his bizarre, DRA-exploding season; after the experience he settled down to productive, if not residential, stability. ⓑ A below-average reliever for the past few years, there might be fewer than 10 people in the country who realized **Javy Guerra** pitched for the Marlins last season. ⓑ Beware the back-end starter who is always one tertiary offering/tweaked delivery/sub-3.00 ERA over half a season in Double-A away from making it big. After stabilizing a haphazard walk rate, former first-round pick **Jon Harris** finally pitched his way up to Triple-A, where he'll try to prove himself a rare exception to the norm yet again. ⓑ **Zachary Jackson** chewed his way through the Blue Jays' farm system with the voracious appetite of a caterpillar preparing for pupal transformation, finally stopping to gnaw on Double-A for a full year while he touched up a plus fastball-curve offering—at least when he knew where it was going. ⓑ It's fairly uncommon for a team to spent two high draft picks on prep players from the same high school, but **Adam Kloffenstein**, Jordan Groshans' teammate at Magnolia High, and his large frame and fastball passed up a TCU commitment for his $2.5 million bonus. ⓑ Add Tommy John recovery to **Elieser Medrano**'s laundry list in 2019, right up there with refining the consistency of his mid-90s heater, tightening the command on his slider and developing a solid third offering within his limited pitch repertoire. ⓑ When we last saw **Julian Merryweather** in 2017, he was a 25-year-old back-end starter who'd mastered but not dominated Double-A and gotten kicked around Triple-A. He lost all of 2018 to Tommy John Surgery, which ... well, it doesn't help. ⓑ The Florida State League's Pitcher of the Year, fireballer **Patrick Murphy** is finally on a path to overcome the law most closely associated with his name—the 2013 draft pick has already undergone thoracic outlet syndrome and Tommy John surgeries. ⓑ Scouts dream on **Hector Perez**'s stuff already plus raw stuff jumping up in short bursts, which is great news considering he doesn't currently have the control or command to stick as a starter. ⓑ "**David Phelps**", the Mariners answered when asked who would get the ball to Edwin Diaz. "Dave Phelps, Dave Phelps, Dave Phelps." Instead his year was lost to injury and rehab. One certainly hopes he fully recovers. After all, people say he has a cannon for an arm. ⓑ Breaking ball specialist **Trent Thornton** was a casualty of the annual pre-Rule 5 shuffle, moving from Houston's crowded 40-man roster to Toronto's more flexible crop in exchange for Aledmys Diaz. ⓑ When **Jacob Waguespack** was traded from the Phillies to the Blue Jays at the deadline for Aaron Loup, he only needed to travel about 250 feet to find his new teammates, as both Triple-A affiliates were squaring off at Lehigh Valley. Familiarity begets familiarity, though, and the potential up-and-down arm rung up his former teammates for a season-high 12 punchouts two days later. ⓧ Still a one-trick pony (large-frame flamethrower with starter potential), **T.J. Zeuch** dodged the injuries that derailed his 2017 season and acquired two more tricks along the way: a potent, if occasionally erratic sinker and slider that play off each other for a convincing double act.

Blue Jays Prospects

The State of the System:
Okay Mark, it's probably a top five system.

The Top Ten:

1   **Vladimir Guerrero Jr.**   **3B**   OFP: 80   Likely: 70
ETA: Whenever Shapiro deigns to make a phone call
Born: 03/16/99   Age: 20   Bats: R   Throws: R   Height: 6'1"   Weight: 200
Origin: International Free Agent, 2015

The Report: A scout once told me that 8 reports are just 2 reports, but longer. How much is there to explain? The usual language of baseball scouting is insufficient. Vladito "came back to earth" in Buffalo, which means that the 19-year-old didn't quite manage to hit [expletive deleted] .400 for a full season in the upper minors. Shruggie face. I spent a soupcon of tortured prose on him already this year. What else is there to say? I shouldn't be writing this blurb. Vladito should belong to the MLB scribes now; let them consult their muses and thesauruses to try to come up with something novel.

He's 7 hit/7 power. Well, that might be low. It's what I can *responsibly* put down on the page. He's a below-average third baseman, but playable there for now if you were so inclined. Get his bat into the lineup however you [expletive deleted] want. This is the best prospect in baseball, the best pure bat in the minors. And the only reason we aren't calling him one of the best pure bats in the majors is we've codified a bunch of sabermetric writing by dudes from 2009 who thought they were smarter than Brian Sabean as "good process." The only good process here is watching Vladito hit majestic dingers on the biggest possible stage. That's what's best for the Blue Jays and best for the game.

The Risks: Low. Yeah, I know. But it's low.

Ben Carsley's Fantasy Take: Listen, writing about fantasy prospects makes one prone to hyperbole. Because everyone is always looking for The Next Star (seriously we were getting "who is the next Ronald Acuna?" questions last February), you feel pressure to exaggerate how good or how impactful guys can be. But the reality of the situation is the established elite tier at pretty much every position is considered elite for a reason. There isn't always an Acuna or a Juan Soto waiting in the wings. Sometimes it's smarter to preach caution and be realistic, even if it's less fun. Sometimes.

This is not that time. Vlad's fantasy ceiling is legitimately as the next Miguel Cabrera. His floor probably looks something like your median Anthony Rizzo year. He's gonna win you a few championships if you're lucky enough to have him/don't suck at roster construction. Let's party.

2 Bo Bichette   SS   OFP: 70   Likely: 60
ETA: Well, I expect he will be ready by late 2019
Born: 03/05/98   Age: 21   Bats: R   Throws: R   Height: 6'0"   Weight: 200
Origin: Round 2, 2016 Draft (#66 overall)

The Report: Dante's kid wasn't quite the same inferno at the plate this year, but Double-A wasn't much of a challenge for him either. Bichette combines elite bat speed and hand/eye to produce a laser show only matched by Pink Floyd Night at your local Planetarium. I don't really buy Bichette's listed height/weight, as his frame looks smaller than listed, but regardless, the plus raw is legit. The ball jumps off his bat and the power plays foul line to foul line. He has so much bat speed that he can really let the ball eat and drive it the other way, and if he does end up at his listed size, there might be more power coming.

Bichette's swing is unorthodox, featuring a long load behind his back shoulder with a near armbar and hitch, but he makes it work and tracks pitches well. He can get too aggressive and pull-happy at the plate, but the raw material is certainly here for a plus-or-better major-league hit tool. At shortstop, Bichette grinds it out to get to fringe-average, but he grows on you there. He has good hands and instincts, but the range is a little light and puts pressure on a merely solid-average arm. Everything just feels a half-grade short for the 6, but then you will see him make a plus play and talk yourself into him sticking there for a while. If he slides over to the keystone, he will be an above-average defender there. But really, you're here for the bat, and there's all-star upside in the profile if Bichette continues to rake in the majors.

The Risks: Medium. I believe in the bat here—although it took a little cajoling—but any swing this unorthodox may allow major league pitchers to suss out holes.

Ben Carsley's Fantasy Take: Did you enjoy Xander Bogaerts' 2018 season? Yes? Good, because that's the type of upside Bichette brings to the table. It's tough to say whether Toronto's absurd... let's call it "caution" with Vladito means they'll hold Bichette down too long as well. But regardless of when Bichette gets the call, he'll be an immediate fantasy factor and potential top-7 fantasy shortstop. He gets lost a bit because he's not the best dynasty prospect in his own organization (Vladito) or at his position (Tatis Jr.), but Bichette is a no-s*** top-10 fantasy prospect right now in his own right. Get excited.

3. Nate Pearson   RHP   OFP: 60   Likely: 50   ETA: 2020
Born: 08/20/96   Age: 22   Bats: R   Throws: R   Height: 6'6"   Weight: 245
Origin: Round 1, 2017 Draft (#28 overall)

The Report: One of the absolute best arms in the minors. He hits 100 MPH with some frequency as a starter, and was famously up to 103-104 with the fastball for a short burst in this year's Fall Stars Game. He's got one of those low-90s sliders that should be a physical impossibility, and a slower curve and change that both flash average-to-plus. It's not just a starter's arsenal, it's a straight-up ace arsenal. The stuff comes packaged in a starter's frame and a pitching motion that doesn't scream reliever. If Pearson fully actualizes, he'll look a lot like another Blue Jays late-first rounder: Noah Syndergaard.

That's the positive side. The negative side starts with some simple math: 20 1/3 of his 42 professional innings were in this year's Arizona Fall League. As a pro, he's been unavailable to pitch far more often than he's been available; before wowing everyone in the AFL, he had a lost 2018 season, with an oblique injury followed by a fractured right forearm from a comebacker in his only regular season start. The delivery isn't totally clean, with a head whack and a fairly hard landing. The fastball can get kind of flat—Peter Alonso turned around one of those 104s for a monster home run. He is going to need one of those offspeed pitches to jump. He's thrown less than two innings in full-season ball, so it isn't like there's a track record of pro success here... yet.

The Risks: Extreme in both directions. Pearson already had significant reliever and injury risks when he was drafted, and a traumatic injury to his pitching forearm didn't reduce those. He has a screw in his pitching elbow from surgery during high school. He could go a lot of different ways in 2019, including paths where the above roles look silly in either direction.

Ben Carsley's Fantasy Take: Eovaldi isn't just a good comp for Pearson's MLB value; it works for his fantasy value as well. That means some years you could be getting a dominating, strikeout-heavy SP3, while other years you could be signing up for an occupied DL slot. In general fantasy owners root for pitchers to remain starters, but in Pearson's case, a future as a closer may be most lucrative.

4. Danny Jansen   C   OFP: 60   Likely: 50   ETA: Debuted in 2018
Born: 04/15/95   Age: 24   Bats: R   Throws: R   Height: 6'2"   Weight: 225
Origin: Round 16, 2013 Draft (#475 overall)

The Report: Warby Parker would struggle to find a better celebrity endorser than Danny Jansen. Besides having some of the most fashionable specs in pro ball, the new lenses sparked a 2017 breakout that continued throughout 2018. It's a striking infomercial before and after: from org guy to borderline Top 101 prospect. Jansen has a bit of an unorthodox swing, where he drops his hands by his hip during setup, followed by a minimal load and a slight uppercut plane. His hand-eye is good enough now that he can still cover just about everything.

The quality of contact is inconsistent, but hard enough to project average hit and power tools, which would make him one of the better hitting catchers in today's game. His glove behind the plate has improved to averageish as well. There are no real weaknesses in his defensive profile, but it's possible he might end up in more of a timeshare if his org prefers a backstop with a plus glove.

The Risks: Low. The balanced profile and 2018 major league performance makes him a fairly safe bet to have a significant major league career.

Ben Carsley's Fantasy Take: I've written at length about how trusting catching prospects to make immediate impacts is a poor strategy. It's through the lens of those lessons learned–and not through any particular fault of Jansen's–that I'm going to urge caution in projecting big 2019 production. Yes, he's close to the majors, and yes, the power tool looks real. But Russell Martin is still going to get plenty of playing time, and the learning curve for young catchers is especially steep. Eventually, Jansen can be a top-10 option and routine 20-homer threat at the position. Just don't confuse his MLB ETA (pretty much right now) with his fantasy impact ETA (2020 or beyond).

5. Kevin Smith   IF   OFP: 55   Likely: 50   ETA: 2020
Born: 07/04/96   Age: 22   Bats: R   Throws: R   Height: 6'1"   Weight: 188
Origin: Round 4, 2017 Draft (#129 overall)

The Report: If not for Vladito, you could make the case that Smith had the most impressive 2018 season among all Blue Jays farmhands. He put to bed the notion that he was a glove-first guy who lacked an approach at the plate by slashing .302/.358/.528 over two levels. The former Maryland star has quick hands, above-average bat speed, and a swing that gets leverage. It's a strong enough bat with above-average raw power that will play at any spot in the infield.

Smith is fluid and balanced defensively, with good instincts and adequate arm strength. It's not flashy but he should stick at short for the foreseeable future. Vladito and Bichette are the future stars of the organization, but Smith is an important cog in the rebuild as well.

The Risks: Medium. He's yet to face advanced pitching in the upper minors and there is bound to be a learning curve there. He has a broad base of skills, however, and that should carry him to the major leagues.

Ben Carsley's Fantasy Take: Smith may be a better IRL prospect than a fantasy one thanks to his defensive profile, but he's still got plenty of value in our world, too. The hope is that Smith continues to hit as he climbs the MiLB ladder and that we eventually view him somewhat similarly to how we see Luis Urias today. Even if the hit tool falls a bit short of those levels, Smith is a nice grab for those of you in deeper leagues today and could hit the back of the top-101 in 2020 if he keeps performing and has as clear a path to playing time as he does at present.

6. Eric Pardinho   RHP

OFP: 60   Likely: 45   ETA: 2023
Born: 01/05/01   Age: 18   Bats: R   Throws: R   Height: 5'10"   Weight: 155
Origin: International Free Agent, 2018

The Report: Pardinho rose to fame as an interesting curiosity in September 2016, when he was the 15-year-old ace of the Brazilian national team in WBC qualifying. Besides being a fun story, he's also a legitimate prospect. Pardinho's signing bonus in the 2017-18 international pool was lower than you might expect for a higher-end J2 with name value, likely because of perceived limited projectability due to his small stature and questions about the level of competition he faced in Brazil. His 2018 pro debut couldn't have been more splendid, with a dominant age-17 season in the Appalachian League against much older batters (Wander Franco excepted). He's incredibly advanced for his age, with significantly better command than you'd expect to see out of his age cohort—high school juniors—and the makings of a full four-pitch mix. He's not a finesse pitcher, either, as he's already running his fastball into the mid-90s. And he's so young.

The Risks: Extreme. He's a 17-year-old short righty in rookie ball. He's here because the stuff profile is so advanced, but he's still a 17-year-old short righty in rookie ball. He might get hurt, he might not be a starter, etc. Quite a lot happens developmentally to young pitchers between rookie ball in the majors.

Ben Carsley's Fantasy Take: Watch list. The top part of your watch list that you fill with players you check in on every 10-or-so days, but still, watch list.

7. Sean Reid-Foley   RHP

OFP: 55   Likely: 45   ETA: Debuted in 2018
Born: 08/30/95   Age: 23   Bats: R   Throws: R   Height: 6'3"   Weight: 220
Origin: Round 2, 2014 Draft (#49 overall)

The Report: The Top 101 version of Reid-Foley showed up more often in 2018, although he remains a frustrating pitching prospect. He'll show a tick-above-average fastball velocity, but it can take him a bit to ramp up to it. Reid-Foley will cut and run the pitch, but it's not always effective movement. He still struggles to show even average command with it, as he tends to lose his release point despite relatively simple mechanics.

Both his breaking balls project as average but will flash better. The slider sits in the mid-80s and will flash good tilt, but it's built to entice grounders rather than swings and misses. The curve comes in around 80 and can bleed into the slider in the low-80s, but Reid-Foley will flash a tight downer version as well. He commands both breakers better than the fastball. His change is used sparingly and can lack deception, but will flash good velo separation and fade. His 2018 major league cameo didn't really answer the main question with the profile, which is "will he throw enough strikes, or enough quality strikes to turn over a lineup multiple times?" The stuff is more solid-average than plus, so Reid-Foley will need to limit the self-inflicted damage to stick in the back of a rotation over the long haul.

The Risks: Low. Reid-Foley finally conquered the upper minors and missed bats everywhere. How much further he refines his command will determine the ultimate major league outcome here. I'd bet he'll always be a little bit frustrating though.

Ben Carsley's Fantasy Take: If Reid-Foley had even marginally better stuff or marginally better command, it'd be a lot easier to get excited about him. As he stands currently, he'll bring much more value to the Jays than he will to fantasy owners. He should be owned in TDGX-sized leagues (800-plus players), but he's a spot starter in shallower formats.

8. Anthony Alford   OF   OFP: 55   Likely: 45   ETA: Debuted in 2017
Born: 07/20/94   Age: 24   Bats: R   Throws: R   Height: 6'1"   Weight: 215
Origin: Round 3, 2012 Draft (#112 overall)

The Report: It's been quite a road. The Blue Jays drafted Alford back in 2012 as a multi-sport star planning to play football at Southern Miss, where he became a part-time starter as a true freshman option quarterback. He transferred to Ole Miss to play defensive back after being charged in a campus altercation, and didn't play much baseball for three seasons until he quit football in the fall of 2014. He quickly re-established himself as a top prospect on the diamond, making the 101 in each of the last three seasons. He has the incredible all-around athletic ability you'd expect of a guy who saw substantial playing time as an FBS true freshman option quarterback.

Alford's baseball career has been marred by a series of injuries, including a severe concussion, a broken hamate, recurring knee problems, and this year's entry, a hamstring strain in spring training. With only 430 pro games under his belt, frankly, he just hasn't played all that much. His hitting performance has been inconsistent, and despite call-ups in each of the last two years, he's yet to master Triple-A. He hasn't hit for much game power to date, although we still think he has enough raw to have a shot at average or even above-average power later on. At times the hit tool has looked like a plus, and at times he's hit in the .230s. His defense is more than good enough for center currently and he can play the corners well, too.

The Risks: High, especially considering that he's spent parts of the last two seasons in the majors. He might not hit and he might not be healthy enough. We're basically giving Alford a pass from his lost 2018 because of his overwhelming athleticism, the history of prior success, and the hamstring injury, but maybe this is what he is now.

Ben Carsley's Fantasy Take: Fool me three times, shame on you, but fool me four times... There's an argument to rank Alford in the Top 101 again based on his speed and proximity to the majors, but I'm out. He can't stay healthy, and I'm not totally convinced he can hit. Will Alford sneak in a few seasons where he swipes 20-plus bases and makes me look dumb? Yep. Will he have even more years where he's a total fantasy non-factor? Also yep.

9. Jordan Groshans SS

OFP: 55 Likely: 45 ETA: 2022
Born: 11/10/99 Age: 19 Bats: R Throws: R Height: 6'3" Weight: 178
Origin: Round 1, 2018 Draft (#12 overall)

The Report: The first of two Magnolia High alums taken by the Jays in last summer's draft, Groshans is a big ol' Texas country boy with country strength to match (yes, yes Magnolia is a sleepy Houston suburb, but let's not let that get in the way of scouting cliches, I have a word count to hit). For now, Toronto has him splitting time between shortstop and third base. The former seems... optimistic given his frame, but his strong arm will play at either spot on the left side of the infield and he has solid enough hands for the hot corner. The body might not cooperate there in five years either, but further physical projection might also allow Groshans to grow into even more raw power. It's plus at present, although he struggles to get to it at times due to a fairly flat swing plane. There's a bit of length to the swing, and an occasional bat wrap sporadically lengthens it further. The profile will require more basting than your average high-pick prep bat, but Groshans could be an above-average regular when the timer goes off.

The Risks: High. Hit tool questions, positional questions, limited pro track record, basically the Full Monty.

Ben Carsley's Fantasy Take: Groshans may not be among the first 10 guys you pop in dynasty first-year player drafts, but he should probably be among the next 10. A three-plus season lead time isn't wonderful, but Groshans has the power and hit projections needed to turn into a top-12 fantasy third baseman in time. Factor in how well the Jays have developed guys like this lately, and there's more to like here from a fantasy perspective than first meets the eye.

10. T.J. Zeuch RHP

OFP: 55 Likely: 45 ETA: Summer 2019
Born: 08/01/95 Age: 23 Bats: R Throws: R Height: 6'7" Weight: 225
Origin: Round 1, 2016 Draft (#21 overall)

The Report: So this fellow is a giant former first-rounder who throws a plus sinker and flashes three offspeed pitches at above-average or better, and has useful command often enough. What is he doing all the way down here? Well, there's a hard reality about the modern game, in that you can have a 60 fastball and two average offspeed pitches without really having a swing-and-miss offering. This has already manifested in Zeuch's poor strikeout rates. The other issue is that his command profile, slider, curve, and change all come and go from look-to-look. He's consistently shown enough to get outs but he hasn't been dominant as often as you'd like. Tall pitchers do sometimes develop late, and there are enough individual pieces here for optimism.

The Risks: Moderate, in that he could just be a sixth starter or middle reliever. There's also more positive risk than you'd think for a 23-year-old college pitcher—there are worse upside bets than the tall dude with this kind of pitch profile.

Ben Carsley's Fantasy Take: Zeuch has just enough upside to be more interesting than most mid-to-backend starter prospects, but that's damning with faint praise. Toronto is not a good place to pitch, Zeuch looks likely to kill your WHIP at present and wins may be hard to come by as a Jay for a good little while. He's a watch list player at best.

The Next Five:

11 Cavan Biggio   IF
Born: 04/11/95   Age: 24   Bats: L   Throws: R   Height: 6'1"   Weight: 203
Origin: Round 5, 2016 Draft (#162 overall)

The other, other, other bloodlines guy at New Hampshire this year, Biggio may not have the upside of Bichette or Vladito, nor the major league time under his belt of Gurriel, but his 2018 was a bit of a minor breakout. While he'd be far from the first lefty to have a power spike playing his home games at Northeast Delta Dental Stadium, Biggio was actually better on the road in 2018. He tweaked his swing to tap into his solid-average raw power and has turned into a potential three-true-outcomes infielder. Where he ends up on the dirt is an intriguing question. He'd be fringy at second or third, but could handle either spot (the aforementioned existence of Vladito, Bichette, and Gurriel meant he played a fair bit of first as well), and while it's not out of the question that he slugs and walks his way to a second-division starter role at one of those spots, Biggio might be best suited as a Swiss Army knife lefty bench piece with some pop. The Blue Jays have started getting him some corner outfield reps as well, perhaps with an eye toward that outcome.

12 Adam Kloffenstein   RHP
Born: 08/25/00   Age: 18   Bats: R   Throws: R   Height: 6'5"   Weight: 243
Origin: Round 3, 2018 Draft (#88 overall)

Groshans' high school teammate got 2.5 million bucks to forgo TCU. Unlike most prep arms, Kloffenstein doesn't need any late-night runs to Raising Cane's to fill out his frame. He's already built like a rotation stalwart, and most of the rest of the profile fits the "third-round overslot prep arm" mold. He's got a fastball that can touch the mid-90s and features wicked two-seam action at times. He has two breaking balls that bleed together a bit, but he'll flash a tight power slider. The change-up is a "work in progress." There's some reliever risk here; compact arm action, Kloffenstein has significant effort in his delivery. Still, given the present stuff and frame, he's a fairly "safe" prep arm—which is to say, not safe at all, but relatively safe.

13 Griffin Conine   OF
Born: 07/11/97   Age: 21   Bats: L   Throws: R   Height: 6'1"   Weight: 200
Origin: Round 2, 2018 Draft (#52 overall)

The other, other, other, other bloodlines guy in the Jays system, Conine was a potential first-round pick coming into his junior year at Duke, but struggled a bit the first half of the season as he sold out for power too much. When you have plus-plus raw, fair enough, but the strikeouts mounted. While he toned it down and his overall line ended up quite robust, concerns about the—at times—controlled violence in his swing may have led to a bit of a draft day slide. The K's and bombs continued apace in his pro career, and he's limited to an outfield corner, so the bombs will have to come pretty regularly. But there's enough juice in the bat to project a potential regular with time. Conine will also miss the first 50 games of 2019 after testing positive for a banned stimulant.

14 Hector Perez   RHP
Born: 06/06/96   Age: 23   Bats: R   Throws: R   Height: 6'3"   Weight: 190
Origin: International Free Agent, 2014

Hey, it's a 95-and-a-slider dude! Perez can actually touch higher in short bursts which might portend more consistent upper-90s velo if he moves to the bullpen, which… he probably will. The arm action is compact but a bit violent, and he's struggled with both his control and command as a starter. He pairs the fastball with a tight, power slider that also carries plus projection. It's potential impact stuff in relief, and Perez could hit the majors in 2019, assuming he can get the walk rate even marginally more under control.

15 Thomas Pannone   LHP
Born: 04/28/94   Age: 25   Bats: L   Throws: L   Height: 6'0"   Weight: 195
Origin: Round 9, 2013 Draft (#261 overall)

I should know better by now than to buy-in to another strike-throwing southpaw sitting in the high-80s with average secondaries after some upper-minors (and even major-league) success. And that's even before we consider that Pannone will have to get by with that profile in the AL East, playing his home games in the Rogers Centre. This profile has fine margins, and while some of these dudes have real major league careers, they also account for a plurality of starters in the upper minors. So your hit rate isn't going to be good.

But I've always liked Pannone more than I should. Some of these guys do make it for a few years after all, and he can hit all four quadrants with the fastball. He hides it a bit, runs it a bit. He's got a big, slow, sweepy curve in the low-70s that he can manipulate, spot or bury. There's good feel for an average change. Pannone might give up a million home runs in the majors, but he's already in the majors, and for whatever reason I think he can be a backend starter or swing guy for a while. These aren't really pref lists, except when they are kinda sorta pref lists.

Others of note:

Logan Warmoth, SS, High-A Dunedin

Certainly on pedigree Warmoth deserves to be ahead of Pannone (and arguably a few other names in the next five), but it's hard to describe his 2018 with anything more polite than "well, it was a lost season." You would expect a polished, 22-year-old college bat to make easy work of the Florida State League, but Warmoth struggled badly. We don't scout the statline of course, but production will matter with this profile, as he doesn't offer much in the way of tools or physical projection. So it would be nice if he'd hit a bit.

The power was always likely to play as below-average, but one home run in a half-season in High-A isn't great, Bob. Warmoth projects as a below-average runner who will have to grind it out at short, and may fit better at third, so an average over .250 would improve our confidence interval w/r/t his being a major-league starter. And yes, Warmoth missed time with hamstring issues, that could be a factor, but he does seem to get hurt a lot. So performance isn't the be all and end all, but it does have to be explained. And none of the explanations I can come up with here are going to be more comforting than "well, it was a lost season."

Jordan Romano, RHP, Triple-A Buffalo

Hey, another 95-and-a-slider dude! Romano is a fine example of how this profile comes from everywhere now—an underslot 10th-rounder out of Oral Roberts in this case. You know the drill: Romano is a big dude who throws in the mid-90s with good command and an average hard slider that flashes better. There's a tad more upside here than you'd think for a guy who just spent the season being good but not great in Double-A at age-25; it took him a few seasons to really get going as a pro due to Tommy John surgery the spring after he was drafted. Whether or not he stays in the rotation depends on the development of his change, which is still fringy. Not the world's most exciting profile, but he's probably going to pitch in the majors for awhile.

Forrest Wall, OF, Double-A New Hampshire

The return from the Rockies for Final Boss, Wall is a former first-round pick who wasn't a disaster in Double-A and was acquired for a pretty good (and cheap) reliever with an additional year of control. He was then not added to the Blue Jays 40-man for Rule 5 protection purposes. Could he stick on another team? Perhaps. He's a plus runner who's still rough in center at times, but he has the range for it.

The swing still looks good. It's a classic, rotational left-handed stroke, although he looked lost at times against Double-A stuff. He lacks physicality... wait, do I just see Carlos Tocci in every prospect now? That's not a great comp, but it might be what Wall does if he's jumped to the majors. And you may not get more than a fourth outfielder at the end of his now-disrupted development process. Unless you are 95-with-a-slider (his arm is fringy and would force him to left if he can't stick up the middle), teams are going to try and sneak you through an extra year now.

Top Talents 25 and Under (born 4/1/93 or later):

1. Vladimir Guerrero Jr.
2. Bo Bichette
3. Nate Pearson
4. Danny Jansen
5. Kevin Smith
6. Ryan Borucki
7. Lourdes Gurriel
8. Eric Pardinho
9. Sean Reid-Foley
10. Anthony Alford

In each of the last two years, this space has led off by noting that hey, the Blue Jays sure are old. It would be poor storytelling for me to not complete the trilogy; at an average of 30.3 years of age, Toronto was indeed old as all heck in 2018. They were also, for the second consecutive year, bad. Old and bad are perhaps the two worst conjoined traits for a baseball team, and fortunately, Mark Shapiro and company have been busy behind the scenes.

Like the planet of Tatooine, the view of Toronto's 25U talent is dominated by the beauty and scorching heat coming off twin stars. Vlad Guerrero Jr. is maybe the only teenager in the history of the game for whom hitting .330 in Triple-A feels anticlimactic, while Bo Bichette is just your standard 20-year-old handling Double-A with aplomb. For some franchises, having either of the two would be a once-a-decade kind of developmental coup. The Blue Jays have both, and the ceiling of the franchise's next era feels inexorably linked to their two stud prospects.

Toronto Blue Jays 2019

Below the headliners, Toronto's youngsters flash talent across positions and levels. Nate Pearson is a huge arm attached to a huge body, coming off a lost season. Kevin Smith is a slick fielding shortstop whose bat serves as another encouraging sign of the org's ability to develop talent. Ditto Danny Jansen, who in two years has progressed from organizational afterthought to Russell Martin's successor-in-waiting.

The last half of the list darts all over the map. Ryan Borucki harnessed his spectacularly whelming profile into spectacularly whelming big-league results, which is worth more than most fans give it credit for. Lourdes Gurriel was the most difficult talent to rank on this list. His prospect hype has waned, and his defense doesn't make him enough of an asset to offset the fact that he walks and dingers just a bit less than needed to be anything more than adequate with the bat. Still, he's a big leaguer, and given that MLB stalwarts like Aaron Sanchez and Marcus Stroman have aged out of consideration for this list, Gurriel settles in at seven here.

Eric Pardinho is barely old enough to drive, and won't reach Toronto until well into the next decade, but his international pedigree and signing bonus, coupled with the faces his fastball melted off in rookie ball, squeak him onto the list. Sean Reid-Foley climbed through three levels in 2018, including Toronto, and missed bats at every level. Anthony Alford has showcased droolworthy tools for years, but has yet to put it all together. His ceiling as a plus CF and accompanying athleticism is all that keeps him on this list—and less athletic players like Billy McKinney, and Reese McGuire off of it.

Fans of the Legion of Adult Large Sons will scream for Rowdy Tellez to be on here, and it's an understandable ask; barrel-shaped boys finding barrel is an aesthetic delight. However, Tallez's underwhelming performance in two seasons of Triple-A make his marginal success in the bigs last September look flukier than we'd like, and his defensive and baserunning skills are, uh, not great.

The 2015-16 Blue Jays were the most entertaining and successful Canadian team in decades, but they were an old club with a short shelf life. The stagnation and ultimate dissolution of that talent stings; saying goodbye to heroes always does. But while 2019 will be a rebuilding year, the farm system looks ready to graduate at least one, and perhaps two legitimate stars. With unrivaled top end prospect depth, and some fun guys coming up behind them, next year's Blue Jays will at least let fans dream of the future, a welcome improvement over mourning the death of their recent past.

Part 3: Featured Articles

The Hole in The Shift is Fixing Itself

Russell Carleton

I've been on a bit of a mission against The Shift of late. I'm not out to get The Shift for the usual reasons that people oppose it. The words "the right way to play the game" won't be found on my lips. If a team wants to pursue a strategy that is within the rules and it works, then by all means, they have my blessing (not that they need it). Instead, my concern with The Shift is a worry that it doesn't work, or at least that it has a flaw that needs fixing.

The data show that while The Shift does a decent job of preventing singles on balls in play (what it's supposed to do), it also increases the number of walks that happen in front of it, and the number of additional walks outweighs the number of singles saved. It's a problem because you can't throw a guy out if he gets to walk to first base.

But the "why" was important. It seemed that The Shift was changing the way in which pitchers pitched. We saw that there were fewer fastballs thrown in front of The Shift than we might otherwise expect, and that pitchers tended to stay out of the strike zone a little more. Not by a lot. In fact, it might not even be visible to the naked eye. The percentage of pitches that are out of the zone goes from 51.0 to 53.3 from a standard defense (two right/two left) to a full shift (three on one side). That difference stands up even after we control for the types of hitters that get shifted against. And it's enough to drive up the walk rate to where it cancels out the benefits that teams thought they were getting with The Shift... and then some.

But there was some hope. I found that when individual pitchers stayed closer to the in-zone/out-of-zone mix that they used without The Shift on, they could still get the benefits of The Shift without the walk problems. So, in theory, a team could simply figure out a way to convince its pitchers to not fall prey to the walk trap and The Shift would once again be their friend.

It's reasonable to think that some teams might be more hip to this idea than others. Maybe some figured it out a year before the others. Maybe they were better at getting the message across to their pitchers. Or, maybe no one has figured it out yet.

Warning! Gory Mathematical Details Ahead!

I used data from 2015-2017, made available through MLB's data portal, Baseball Savant. They are kind enough to note when teams are using an infield shift (three fielders on one side of second base), as opposed to a "strategic shift" (someone's playing a bit out of position, but it's not quite that drastic) or a "standard" alignment.

Since we're doing this by team, I can't just look at raw walk rates, because we know that some teams have good pitchers and others have not-so-good pitchers. Some have a mix of both. I used the log-odds ratio method to take into account a batter's general walking proclivities, and a pitcher's as well, and then shoving them into a binary logistic regression. Then, I asked the computer to generate a specific coefficient for each team's pitchers, for when they went into The Shift and how that affected their walk rate.

Using those coefficients, I was able to project what would happen if a league-average pitcher faced a league-average hitter (which we expect would produce a league-average walk rate; from 2015-2017, 7.7 percent of plate appearances ended in a walk) and then just switched his hat. Here's the top five and the bottom five:

Top 5 Teams	Projected Shift Walk Rate	Bottom 5 Teams	Projected Shift Walk Rate
Rockies	6.2%	Rangers	11.2%
Pirates	6.7%	Mets	10.4%
Indians	7.2%	Dodgers	10.2%
Astros	7.3%	Cardinals	9.9%
Braves	7.7%	Tigers	9.7%

There are probably people out there right now trying to figure out what the common thread is among the top and bottom teams. I'm sure, because this is Baseball Prospectus, people are already trying to make the case that sabermetric "early adopters" have some sort of edge here. I think that the more interesting piece is that by the time you get to fifth place in The Shift, we're at league average.

As a sanity check, I examined the issue on a pitch-by-pitch level, looking at how often pitchers threw their pitches in the GameDay strike zone, and again using the same basic methodology and getting team-specific coefficients. The names on the list re-arranged themselves, but the idea was the same, and the two lists correlated with an R of .593.

There's a reason that I don't usually do this type of leaderboard post. I don't really know what the Rockies, Pirates, Indians, Astros, and Braves have in common, or what they have that the bottom five don't. I can put a shrug emoji here and say, "Well, it must be something!" but that seems like a cop-out. Instead, I'd like to present another table and suggest that the table above doesn't even really matter anymore.

Year	League Percent Outside K Zone (Full Shift)	League Percent in K Zone (No Shift)	Difference
2015	54.1%	51.1%	3.0%
2016	53.3%	50.9%	2.4%
2017	52.6%	50.9%	1.7%
2018	52.0%	50.7%	1.3%

The hole in The Shift is fixing itself, and it's coming down really fast league wide. In my earlier work on The Shift, I suggested that until teams stopped having such a huge difference between their out-of-zone rate with and without The Shift on, there would just be too many walks for The Shift to make sense. It seems that all 30 of them have been working toward just that. I once estimated that it takes about 10 years for an idea to filter its way through baseball. At this rate, it looks like teams are going to catch up a lot faster than that. And yeah, they're all saber-smart now.

It's likely that whatever magic it was that the Rockies and Pirates had has made its way to Texas and Queens. Or is at least on its way. And if teams are committing to fixing the walk problem, then it's likely that they will continue shifting and shifting a lot.

And eventually it's going to actually make sense for them to do it.

—*Russell Carleton is a former author of Baseball Prospectus and now an analyst for the New York Mets.*

The State of the Quality Start

Rob Mains

One of the seven things you (probably) didn't know about the 2018 season is that quality starts—defined as a start lasting six or more innings with three or fewer earned runs allowed—as a percentage of total starts cratered to an all-time low of 41 percent. I want to look a little more deeply into this, since it's been a while (May of 2016, to be exact) since I've examined quality starts.

The term *quality start* is credited to *Philadelphia Inquirer* sportswriter John Lowe. It's been derided ever since he coined it in December of 1985. Three runs in six innings? That's a 4.50 ERA! In what world is that a measure of quality?

Let's start with that criticism. It's true that 3 x 9 / 6 = 4.5. (You came here for this sort of high-level math, right?) But it's also true that type of start, meeting the bare minimum for earning a quality start, is unusual. Here's the proportion of quality starts in which the pitcher lasted exactly six innings and yielded exactly three earned runs. (I'm going to confine this analysis to the 30-team era, 1998-present. Almost all data retrieved in this article is via the Baseball-Reference Play Index.)

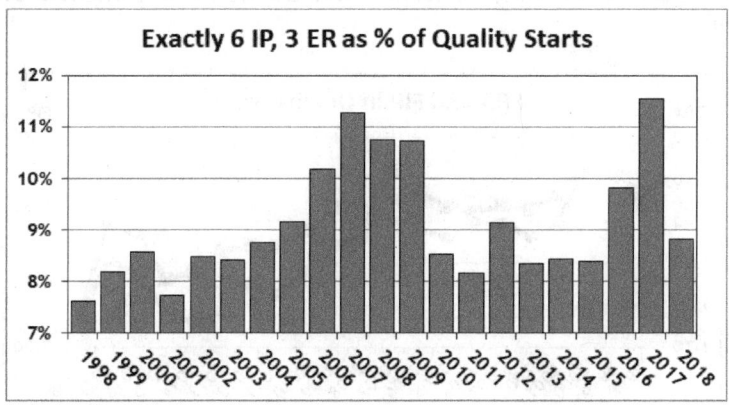

There were 1,997 quality starts in 2018. Only 176, or fewer than one in 11, featured a pitcher going six innings and allowing three earned runs. Put another way, the percentage of quality starts that resulted in a 4.50 ERA (8.8 percent) is less than half the percentage of games in which a batter hit two home runs and his team lost (22.5 percent; 237-69 won-lost). That doesn't impugn hitting two homers.

So if a 4.50 ERA isn't the norm, what is? How good are quality starts?

Pretty good, it turns out. First, on a team level:

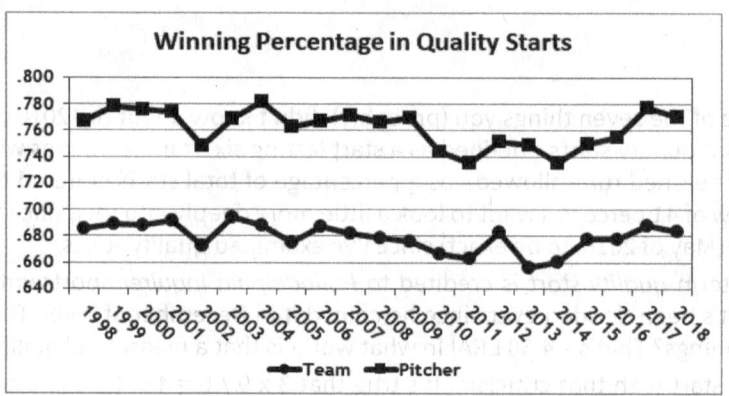

Teams receiving a quality start from their pitcher won 68.4 percent of their games in 2018, in line with the 30-team era average of 67.9 percent. A team with a .684 winning percentage wins 111 games. Getting a quality start is definitely a good thing. Individual pitchers throwing quality starts have a higher winning percentage because a big slice of team losses is assigned to a reliever.

If teams do well in quality starts, how well do the starting pitchers do? Again, very well.

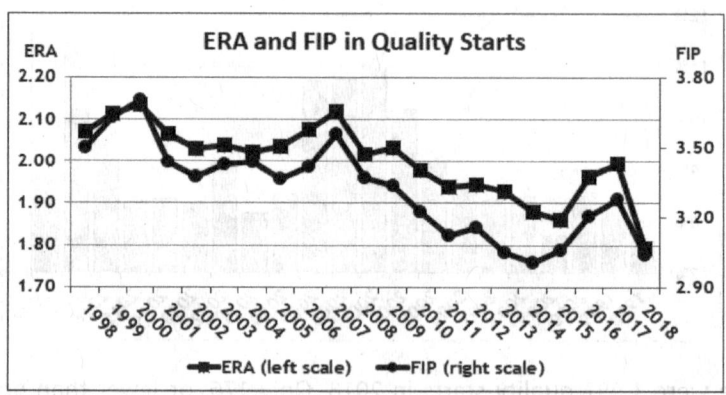

Pitchers in quality starts had a 1.79 ERA (blue line) in 2018, *the lowest in the 30-team era*. Their FIP was higher, 3.04, but still excellent. In the 30-team era, only 2014 had a lower FIP for quality starts, 3.01.

But, of course, the run environment in 2014 was different. Teams in 2014 scored 4.07 runs per game, the fewest in a non-strike year since 1976. They scored 4.45 runs per game in 2018. So surrendering a 3.04 FIP in 2018 is more impressive than 3.01 in 2014. Accordingly, let's look at ERA and FIP in quality starts relative to league averages.

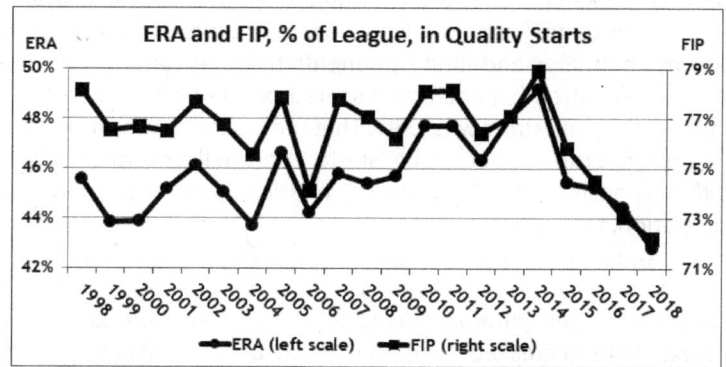

This tells a more dramatic story. Starting pitchers in 2018 gave up a 4.19 ERA and a 4.21 FIP. Starters in quality starts gave up a 1.79 ERA, 43 percent of the league average. Starters in quality starts gave up a 3.04 FIP, 72 percent of the league average. Both of these marks represent lows in the 30-team era.

The takeaway here is this: *Quality starts are better, relative to other starts, than they've ever been over the past 21 years.*

Maybe during the winter I'll look at this over a longer arc of time. For now, though, we can definitively say quality starts are the best they've ever been since the Diamondbacks and Rays joined the majors.

Yet, paradoxically, they're down.

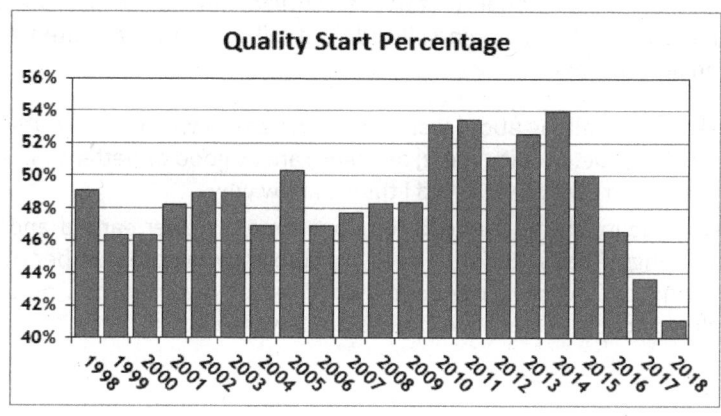

This graph covers only the 30-team era. In my article last week, though, I looked at the years 1908-2018. The result was the same. The 41 percent of starts in 2018 that were quality starts are an all-time low, well below the runners-up: 1930's 43 percent (the year teams scored an all-time record 5.55 runs per game) and last year's 44 percent.

The normal explanation for a dip in quality start percentage is an increase in scoring. When teams score a lot of runs, it's harder for starting pitchers to last six or more innings and limit opponents to three earned runs. From 1998 to 2014, the correlation between runs scored per game and the percentage of starts that were quality starts was -0.94. That means there was an extremely close relationship: More runs, fewer quality starts. Too small a sample? Go back to the start of the Expansion Era, 1961, and the relationship is even more negative, a -0.95 correlation, though 2014.

But that's broken down over the past four years:

- 2015: Runs per game increased from 4.07 to 4.25, quality start percentage decreased from 54.0 to 50.1. Yes, that's a negative relationship, but the regression model would predict a decline of 1.5 percentage points. We got 3.9 instead.
- 2016: Runs per game increased from 4.25 to 4.48, quality start percentage decreased from 50.1 to 46.6. Past experience would suggest a decline of just 1.8 percentage points. We got 3.4.
- 2017: Runs per game increased from 4.48 to 4.65, quality start percentage decreased from 46.6 to 43.6. Again, the direction's right, but the magnitude isn't. Using the relationship from 1998 to 2014, that increase in scoring should've reduced quality starts by 1.3 percentage points, not 2.9.
- 2018: Runs per game declined from 4.65 to 4.45. That should've resulted in the quality start percentage moving in the other direction, rising 1.6 points. It didn't. It fell 2.6 points, as noted, to an all-time low.

Granted, we're talking about just four years here. Maybe they're outliers. But I don't think they are. Quality starts, as noted, are as good or better than ever. But they're rarer than ever as well. And I think I know why.

To get a quality start, you need to allow three or fewer earned and pitch at least six innings. That's 18 outs. Here's a graph showing the number of starting pitchers who limited their opponents to three or fewer earned runs but got pulled after pitching at least five innings but fewer than six:

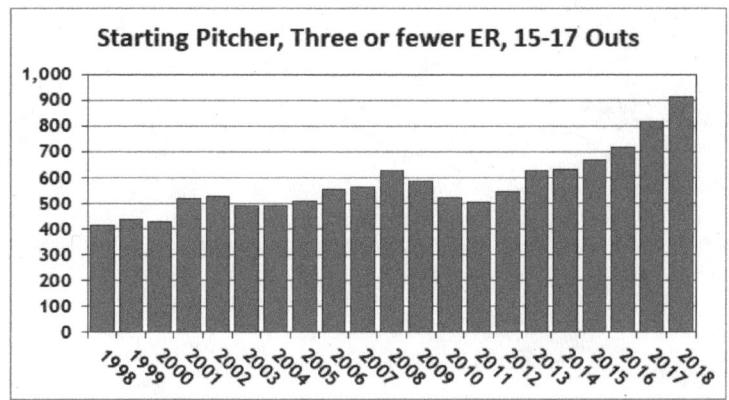

A pitcher getting 15 outs pitched five innings. A pitcher getting 16 outs pitched 5 1/3. A pitcher getting 17 outs pitched 5 2/3. More than ever before, pitchers are being removed from games in which they are within 1-3 outs of a quality start, falling just short of the six-inning finish line. Widespread acknowledgement of the times-through-the-order penalty and a flotilla of available bullpen arms is making the quality start simultaneously both more excellent and more rare.

Which is ironic, given that we saw a new post-war quality start record this season:

Rank	Pitcher	Season	Consecutive QS
1	Jacob deGrom	2018	24
2	Bob Gibson	1968	22
-	Chris Carpenter	2005	22
4	Johan Santana	2004	21
5	Luis Tiant	1968	20
-	Mike Scott	1986	20
-	Jake Arrieta	2015	20
8	Robin Roberts	1952	19
-	Tom Seaver	1973	19
-	Jack Morris	1983	19
-	Greg Maddux	1998	19
-	Josh Johnson	2010	19
-	Jon Lester	2014	19

While there have been longer streaks spread over multiple seasons, no pitcher since World War II threw more consecutive quality starts in one year than Jacob deGrom this year. The fact that he did in a year in which quality starts were the rarest they've ever been adds to the accomplishment.

—*Rob Mains is an author of Baseball Prospectus.*

Heads-Up Hacking—The First Pitch

Matthew Trueblood

Batters fell behind in a higher percentage of all plate appearances in 2018 than in any previous season for which we have pitch-by-pitch data. That kind of granular information goes back only to 1988, but we might safely assume (given all we know about baseball as it had been before that, and as it has been in the years since) that batters have *never* fallen behind at a higher rate than they did last season.

Through the 1990s, the percentage of all plate appearances that began 0-1 hovered in the high 30s and low 40s. In the 2000s, it rose steadily but slowly, through the mid-40s. In 2018, 49.8 percent of all trips to the plate began 0-1. That, as much as anything, captures in microcosm the nature of hitting in MLB today.

A countdown clock toward strike three begins ticking almost the moment a batter takes his place in the box. The league's adjusted OPS+ on the first pitch was higher in 2018 than ever before, and that has been true in most of the last 10 seasons. Batters hit .264/.289/.442 in all plate appearances in which they swung at the first pitch last season, and .241/.330/.395 in all plate appearances in which they took that first offering.

The percentage differences in batting average and isolated power there favor swinging at the first pitch by more than in any season since 1988, while the difference in on-base percentage favors taking by more than ever. If you want to get on base at a decent clip, it's a good idea to be patient, but you run the risk of missing the only chances you'll get to produce power.

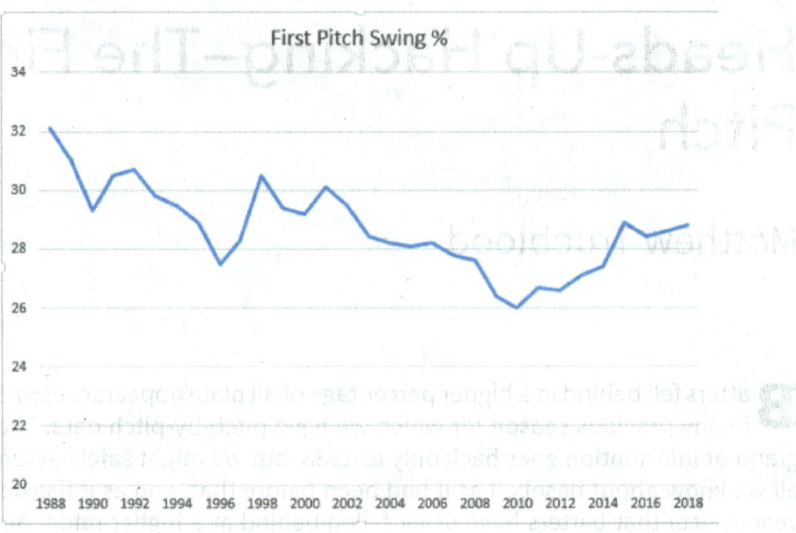

The league swung at the first pitch 28.8 percent of the time in 2018. With the isolated exception of 2015, that's the highest that number has climbed since 2002, but it might not be high enough. With the help of BP research maven Rob McQuown, I looked at the aggregate Called Strike Probability (CSProb) on the first pitch for each season since 2008, when the implementation of PITCHf/x first made measuring that possible. It's risen sharply during that period.

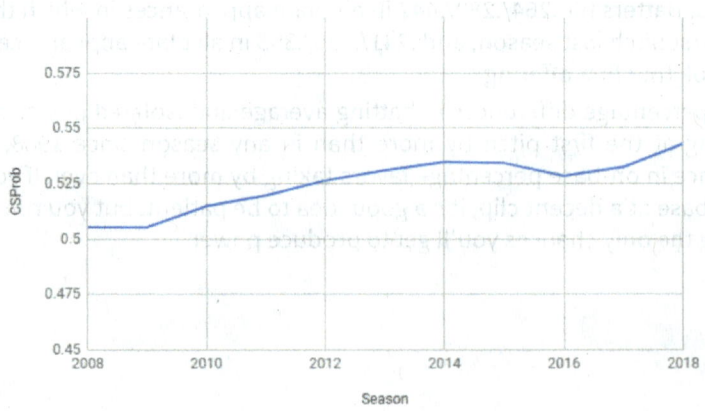

Called Strike Probability, First Pitch of PA (2008-2018)

Called Strike Probability is exactly what it sounds like: a pitch with a given CSProb has roughly that chance of being called a strike, if not swung at. In 2018, a batter who took 100 first pitches from a random sampling of the league's pitchers might expect to fall behind 54 or 55 times—up from 50 or 51 times in 2008. Almost regardless of pitch type (and, notably, especially in the case of fastballs), the first pitch tends to have more of the zone right now than ever before.

Pitchers are better at throwing strikes. They have better stuff, and believe more in their ability to miss bats within the zone. Perhaps most importantly, they know that batters are looking for one thing on the first pitch: a fastball. If they don't get it, they're likely to take the pitch. Check out how the use of sinkers and four-seamers on the first pitch has changed in a decade:

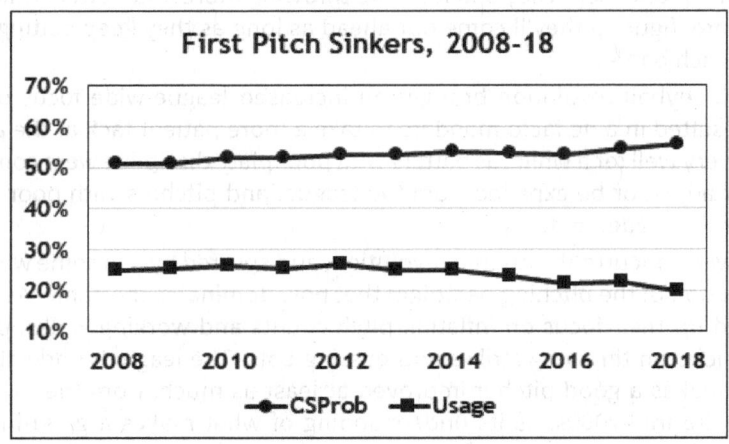

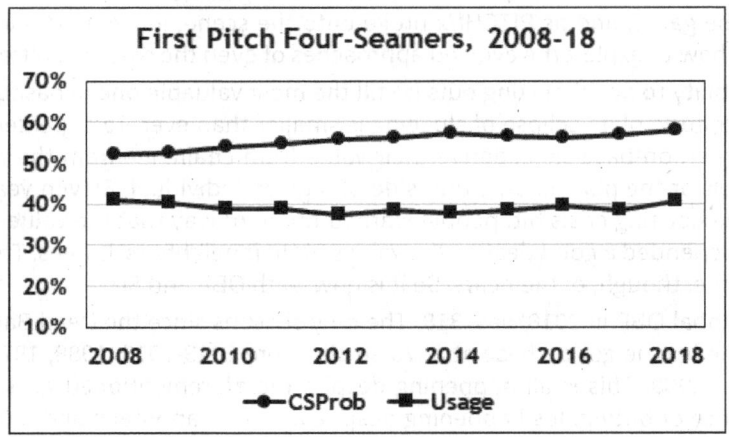

The sinker is losing its place in baseball, but the rate at which pitchers have thrown it on the first pitch hasn't dropped any faster than its usage rate in other counts. Pitchers have actually gone to their four-seamer *more* often to open counts, in the last few years, after a dip in the 2012-2015 period. What's really changed, though, and what shows up in both charts above, is that pitchers are catching more of the zone with first-pitch fastballs than they were a decade ago, or a half-decade ago. They're attacking right away, even with the pitch they know batters are expecting. The message is pretty clear: batters are being too passive.

Sliders, curves, and changeups each have more of the zone when thrown on the first pitch than they did several years ago, too, though the effect is less pronounced. Pitchers have seen the numbers; they know batters are doing better on the first pitch itself. They still feel safe throwing more and better strikes than ever before, figuring they'll come out ahead as long as they keep getting ahead to open each battle.

The Moneyball revolution brought an increased league-wide focus on OBP, which resulted in a de facto mandate to take a more patient tack at the plate. It worked very well for a while, as batters with poor plate discipline were compelled to either adjust or be expelled from the league, and pitchers with poor control were slowly weeded out.

However, concurrent with that revolution, and spurred by it in some ways, was the evolution of the pitching paradigm that now dominates the game. As batters ratcheted up their focus on inflating pitch counts and working walks, pitchers honed theirs on throwing strikes and missing bats. The league's understanding of what makes a good pitcher improved at least as much, from the mid-1990s through the mid-2000s, as its understanding of what makes a good hitter. As amphetamines and other performance-enhancing drugs were phased mostly out of the game, and as PITCHf/x broke onto the scene, individuals and teams learned how to exploit the evolved approaches of even the smartest hitters.

The ability to avoid making outs is still the most valuable one in baseball, but the magnitude of its eclipse of slugging is smaller than ever. To a greater extent than power, on-base skills derive their value from chaining—from the on-base skill levels of the players on either side of a given individual. Eleven years ago, when the housing crisis hit, people learned the hard way that the value of their homes depended a good deal on the values of their neighbors' homes. The same wasn't true, though, of their cars. So it is now, with OBP and SLG.

The global OBP in 2018 was .318. The only seasons since the Dead Ball Era in which the league got on base at a worse clip were 2013-2015, 1988, 1971-1972, and 1963-1968. This is all happening despite the aforementioned evolution of the science of hitting. It's happening despite a shift in approach and focus, one that would steer OBP ever higher, if only it were working.

Instead, it's sitting at a low ebb, and while it does so, even guys who get on base often are a little less helpful than they were 10 years ago—or 20, or 40, or 60, or 70, or 80, or 90. They're less helpful, that is, because unless there happen to be three or four other guys in the lineup who get on just as regularly, their contribution is merely to forestall the inevitable. Runs happen, increasingly, when a sudden bang happens, and that means attacking early in the count—because pitchers are sure as hell doing that.

In a league making contact on barely 75 percent of its swings, and a league in which an increasing number of pitchers can throw multiple off-speed pitches for strikes in any count, the only way to consistently generate offense is going to be aggressive. This isn't necessarily true for individuals, like Mookie Betts and Jose Ramirez, who make a lot of contact and have excellent plate discipline, and whose power comes from such natural quickness in a short stroke. Most players have to make tradeoffs, though, whether it be lowering their contact rate or raising their chase rate, in order to consistently make the quality of contact necessary to survive in today's game.

Highest %	Lowest %
Javier Baez – 48.3	Joe Mauer – 4.6
Freddie Freeman – 47.1	Mookie Betts – 9.7
Ozzie Albies – 46.3	Brett Gardner – 10.7
Jose Altuve – 44.2	Jose Ramirez – 12.0
Nick Castellanos – 44.1	Jason Kipnis – 13.8
Joey Gallo – 42.3	Jesus Aguilar – 14.5
Corey Dickerson – 40.9	Xander Bogaerts – 15.8
Salvador Perez – 40.8	Brian Dozier – 16.3
Eddie Rosario – 40.7	Mike Trout – 17.6
Nick Ahmed – 40.4	Yasmani Grandal – 17.6

Top 10 and Bottom 10 Hitters, First-Pitch Swing Rate (2018)

The question isn't which of these lists one prefers, but what they each convey, qualitatively, about the cat-and-mouse game of early-count hitting. Those top five on the left, especially, drive home the fact that for most players, getting aggressive early in the count is now key to keeping strikeout rate down and hitting for power.

For now, the message is: pitchers are coming right after batters with the nastiest stuff they've ever had. Batters had better stop giving away strike one and force hurlers to adjust, or the global OBP crisis is only going to get worse.

—*Matthew Trueblood is an author of Baseball Prospectus.*

A Hymn for the Index Stat

Patrick Dubuque

We survived without computers. I know this, because I remember the day when my dad hooked up his brand-new Atari 400 computer to the back of our 12-inch Magnavox television, and the perfect blue of the memo pad lit up for the first time. I was born just on the edge of that transitional generation, of learning cursive and balancing checkbooks and just doing math all the time, constant manual arithmetic.

It still amazes me. We learned how to sail ships without computers. We learned how to do calculus. We built towers that didn't fall down, most of the time. We engineered catapults to knock them down anyway. We built a robust system of philosophy called "utilitarianism," founded on the principle that the good of an action is evaluated by summing the effects of that action, which is the kind of formula that would make the world's mainframes crash. The whole foundation of statistics as a field is "here's math you could easily do but would die of old age first."

The fact of the matter is that there is too much math in the world to do. There are too many things changing, and too many things too small to notice, for us to handle. At some point, they become too much for the computers to handle as well, which is why we have chaos theory and undetectable earthquakes, but it's not an even fight. At some point, we fall back on intuition, and given how under-equipped we are, we're forced to bestow that intuition with some sort of supernatural superiority, the "gut feeling," that we can't prove because we can only intuit that our intuition is better.

We're all lousy at intuition, and wonderful at lying to ourselves about it. The honest truth is that computers are far better at intuition than we are, because in order to know what feels "off" you have to know what's "on." In order to do that you have to constantly reassess the average of everything, then re-rank your own experience against it.

Test your own, by comparing these three anonymous lines:

Player	G	HR	AVG	OBP	SLG
Player A	156	38	.259	.342	.535
Player B	154	38	.280	.348	.527
Player C	158	38	.266	.343	.509

These all seem like pretty similar players, right? The second one a touch more batted-ball dependent, the third a little less strong, but all pretty good hitters. And you'd be right, about the latter. Not the former.

Here's the breakdown:

- Player A: 1991 Howard Johnson, 141 DRC+
- Player B: 1996 Dean Palmer, 121 DRC+
- Player C: 2018 Giancarlo Stanton, 114 DRC+

Baseball is fortunate to have escaped the seismic shifts of so many other sports, where the talents and performances of other eras are nearly unrecognizable. (And not just other sports: try to explain the greatness of the movie Duck Soup without adjusting for era.) But they're still there, and they're nearly impossible to account for manually, without having to resort to sweeping generalizations like "steroid era" or juiced-ball era" to throw out entire swathes of production.

This is all to say that we should celebrate the index stat, that simple 100-based scale with such a humble aim: just to give context. It's hard to imagine how we lived without them for so long. Sabermetricians have always tried to make their stats look like other stats: True Average mapped to batting average, FIP molded to look like and compare to ERA. It's easy to understand the motivation—these statistics carry an emotional value in them that is hard to resist, as with the .300 hitter and the 2.00 ERA—but even they fall prey to the same loss of scale as their unadjusted counterparts. If a .300 average means different things in different years, does that hold true for a .300 True Average?

Instead, 100 doesn't say anything, except above average or below. And it does it instantly, for every season in every run environment for any statistic we want it to. We should have more index stats: K%+, so we can stop comparing Mike Clevinger's career 9.46 K/9 to Nolan Ryan's 9.55. HBP%+, so we can note that Ron Hunt was getting plunked when nobody else was getting plunked, as opposed to that imitator Brandon Guyer. Some might note how stale these references are and accuse league-adjustment as a backward-looking drive, and this is true. But we're always looking backward, always comparing the new with the expectations already set. The index stat just forces us to be honest.

There's always resistance to a new statistic, especially one so outwardly simple and so internally complex. We tend to stick with what we know, even in the case of formulas that are supposed to tell us what we know. But if your resistance is that it seems too complicated, too counterintuitive, too "black boxy," I encourage you to consider why you feel that way. Because the real world is infinitely more complicated than baseball, where all the pitches go in one basic direction and the baserunners are only allowed to travel in four directions. Baseball statistics based on mixed methodology are almost impossibly intricate. So are skyscrapers and automobiles. That's why we have computers—to take the guesswork out of them.

—*Patrick Dubuque is an author of Baseball Prospectus.*

Index of Names

Alford, Anthony 79, 102
Axford, John 44
Barnes, Danny 46
Biagini, Joe 49
Bichette, Bo 80, 98
Biggio, Cavan 81, 104
Borucki, Ryan 51
Brito, Ronny 92
Buchholz, Clay 53
Castaneda, Felipe 93
Conine, Griffin 92, 105
Davis, Jonathan 92
Diaz, Yennsy 93
Dillon, Justin 93
Drury, Brandon 18
Galvis, Freddy 20
Gaviglio, Samuel 55
Giles, Ken 57
Grichuk, Randal 22
Groshans, Jordan 92, 103
Guerra, Javy 93
Guerrero Jr., Vladimir 82, 97
Gurriel, Lourdes 24
Hernandez, Teoscar 26
Hiraldo, Miguel 92
Jackson, Zachary 93
Jansen, Danny 28, 99
Kloffenstein, Adam 104
Leiter, Mark 59
Maese, Justin 88
Maile, Luke 92
Mayza, Tim 61
McGuire, Reese 84
McKinney, Billy 30
Morales, Kendrys 32
Murphy, Patrick 93
Norris, Bud 63
Pannone, Thomas 65, 105
Pardinho, Eric 89, 101
Paulino, David 90
Pearson, Nate 91, 99
Pentecost, Max 85
Perez, Hector 93, 105
Pillar, Kevin 34
Pompey, Dalton 86
Reid-Foley, Sean 67, 101
Richard, Clayton 69
Romano, Jordan 106
Sanchez, Aaron 71
Shoemaker, Matt 73
Smith, Kevin 92, 100
Smoak, Justin 36
Sogard, Eric 92
Stroman, Marcus 75
Tellez, Rowdy 38
Tepera, Ryan 77
Thornton, Trent 93
Travis, Devon 40
Urena, Richard 42
Waguespack, Jacob 93
Wall, Forrest 87, 106
Warmoth, Logan 92, 106

Toronto Blue Jays 2019

Zeuch, T.J. 93, 103

Ballpark diagrams for Baseball Prospectus are created by THIRTY81Project, a design concept offering original ballpark artwork, including the new 'Ballparks of 2019' 11 x 17 color print.

Visit **www.thirty81project.com** for full details.

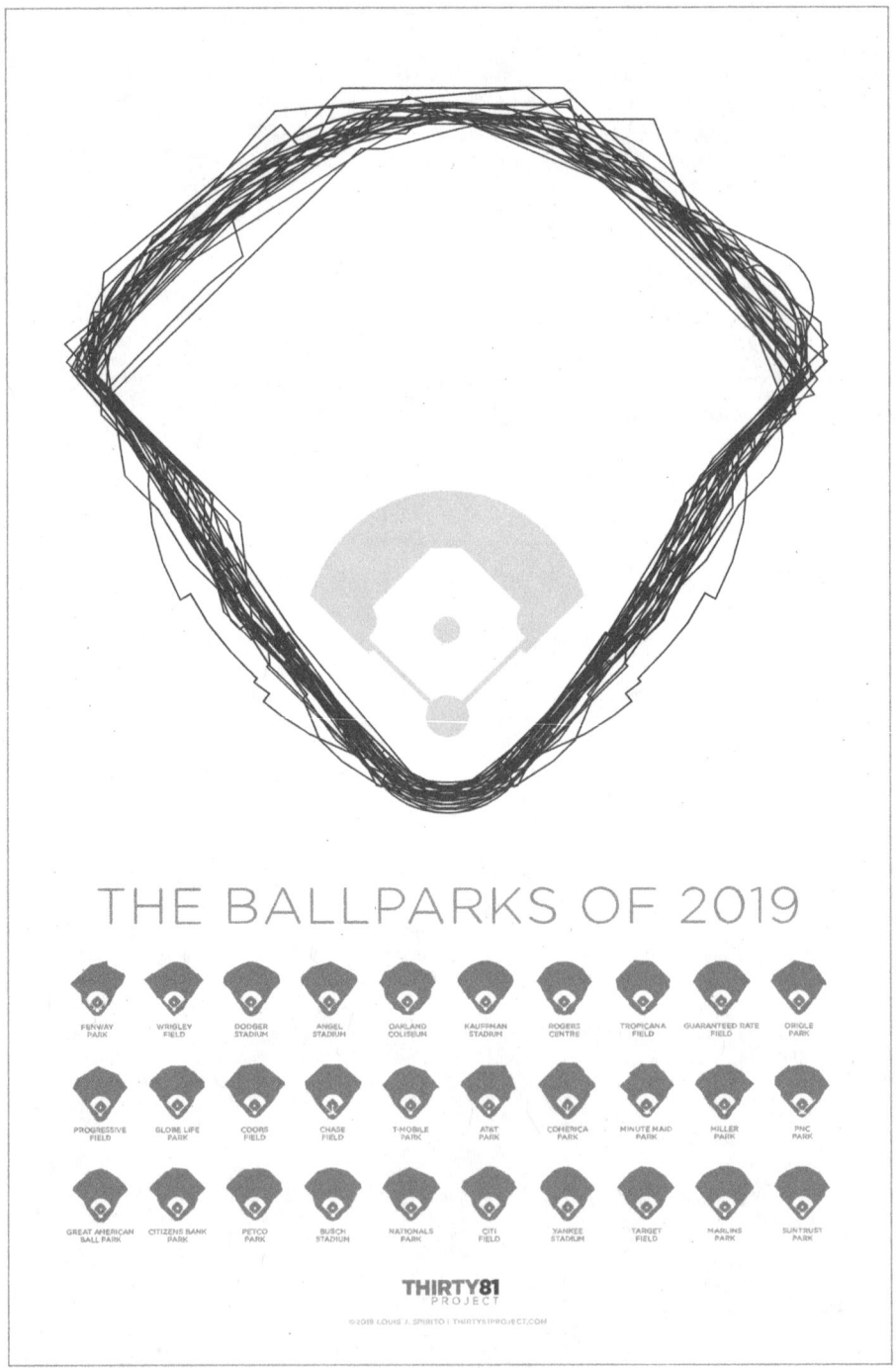